101
WAYS TO BOOST
YOUR CHILD'S
SELF-ESTEEM

101
WAYS TO BOOST
YOUR CHILD'S
SELF-ESTEEM

by Dr. Alvin H. Price, Ph.D.
and Jay A. Parry

Illustrations by Kimble Pendleton Mead

Cover photograph by Barbara Campbell

Design by One Plus One Studio, New York City

ISBN 0-940212-09-9

Printed and bound in the United States of America

Published by American Baby Books

Wauwatosa, WI 53226

Published simultaneously in Canada

This book was created at Information Design, Inc. It was
produced through the joint efforts of:

Larry Belliston—Developer/Planner
Kurt Hanks—Director
Jay A. Parry—Author
Dr. Alvin H. Price—Author
David Bartholomew—Typography
Jill Moffat—Typography
Vicki Parry—Researcher

Distributed in Canada by:
Canadian Baby Books
One Adam Street
Kitchener, Ontario N2H 5P6

CONTENTS

INTRODUCTION

"Is there a magic formula for raising a happy, healthy child?" ask many parents. Of course, magic formulas exist only in fairy tales, but there is something that comes close.

Self-esteem describes how your child feels about himself. Everything your child thinks and does is directly tied to his self-esteem.

Self-esteem is so closely tied to a person's view of life itself that everything she experiences affects her self-esteem, either to build it up or tear it down.

That makes it a dangerously fragile thing, if it's mishandled. But it also makes it the secret magic formula so many parents are looking for: if they can build their child's self-esteem, they've got the battle licked, because they've done something that will positively affect every facet of their child's life.

How do you build self-esteem in a child? There are some basic keys. Help him know he's accepted in the home. Help her have success experiences. Help him know he's important. Help her be capable and competent.

There are countless ways to bring these things into your child's life, and in this book we give you 101. That's really all you need. If you apply the ideas in this book, your child will grow up with a high self-esteem, and you'll have found the magic formula.

But don't think you have to do all 101. The perfect parent doesn't exist, and you'd be near perfect if you did all 101 things in this book. *You don't have to do them all.*

Just choose several of these methods to build your child's self-esteem. Apply them in your home. Make them work for you. Once you have a few working, choose a few more and get going on them.

Building self-esteem is a gradual, ongoing process, and therefore, this book applies to children from infancy to adolescence. Don't just use these suggestions once and forget them; repeat them throughout your child's growing years.

Read through the 101 tips, then, and choose a few to work on. Then choose a few more, and use those tips too. Pretty soon boosting your child's self-esteem will all become a joyous way of life in your home, and the entire family will benefit.

1—YOUR CHILD'S BODY

An important part of good self-esteem is a feeling of acceptance and comfort about one's own body. That feeling comes naturally to a child—unless and until his parent destroys it.

We do our work of destruction in subtle, unspoken ways. Two-year-old Chuck is fondling his penis. Before he knows it, he has an erection. "Oh, no," his dad thinks. "Chuck's starting to masturbate already!" Dad slaps Chuck's hand away.

Patty has an *extremely* messy diaper. (You know the kind—it oozes!) "Ugh," her mom says. "How can you stand it?" She wrinkles her nose while she cleans and changes Patty.

Stan jumps out of the tub and runs into the living room, where mom and dad have company. Their faces turn red, and they chase him back into the bathroom. "Don't be naughty!" his dad says.

Very soon you have three young children who are ashamed and uncomfortable about their bodies. But what is the body? It's the outside of their *selves*. Their shame and discomfort, then, are quickly transferred to their entire beings. They end up with a low self-esteem.

Your child's self-esteem will be bolstered if you help him accept his body and its functions.

You can accomplish this by doing just the opposite of what Chuck's, Patty's, and Stan's mom and dad did. When your child explores his body, accept that as a normal part of growth. If the practice seems to become excessive, distract your child with something else to do.

When your child creates a messy diaper, don't treat his bodily functions with distaste. Be pleasant and cheerful, even though *he* made the mess and *you* have to clean it up.

When he shows his natural lack of inhibitions about nudity, gently put a towel around him or get him dressed. Don't show embarrassment or anger.

The most important thing you can do is have a comfortable attitude about *your* body. Kids can read between the lines. They know what's going on. If you're comfortable, you'll be able to convey that to your child and help him have the self-esteem he deserves to have.

11

2—FOCUS YOUR ATTENTION

Everyone knows that kids thrive on attention. But simple attention isn't all they need. They need a special kind. They need *focused attention*.

Every day give your child your undivided attention to show him that he's genuinely important to you.

How do children feel when they know they're important to their parents? Like they're worth something. Of course I'm talking about self-esteem.

Suppose you went to a movie and only watched it sporadically, spending the rest of the time talking to your partner or out in the lobby getting popcorn. When the movie's over you say, "Gee, that was a poorly done film. I didn't enjoy it a bit."

It's sad to say, but some parents approach child rearing in just this way. When it's time to give attention, they do it only half-heartedly.

Little Ellie burst in through the front door, just home from school. "Hey, Mom! Guess what!"

Mom was washing dishes. What should she do? Ellie's obviously excited—but there's a lot of work to be done. It's a bad time to be interrupted.

But Mom makes the better choice. "What?" she says, smiling. She dries her hands, kneels down beside Ellie, touches her arm, and looks straight into her eyes.

Chances are that Ellie doesn't have anything too important to tell her mother. But something very important *is* going on here: Mom is giving Ellie her *focused attention*.

3—SIMPLIFY THE ENVIRONMENT

The more opportunities for success you can give your child, the better for his self-esteem. One way to assure success is to make the environment such that he won't be continually running up against "failure walls" or "NO! walls."

Aaron wanted to get himself dressed, but the buttons on his shirts were hard to handle—even for his mother. Solution: buy clothes that Aaron could button himself.

But once he had the right clothes, there was another problem: most of the drawers in his dresser were too high for him to reach. Solution: Dad built him a box he could stand on to get his clothes out.

Simplify your child's environment so it fits him better, and he'll be able to have more successes in your home. The more successes he has, the higher his self-esteem will be.

When you think about it, every aspect of our environments is designed for an adult. The closet rods, the door knobs, the beds, the stairs, the kitchen table and chairs, the light switches, the water faucets, the car seats, the toilet seats—they're all designed for you and me but not at all for our younger kids.

Try this experiment. Tonight at supper take a look at how high your child's head pops up over the dining room table. Notice how he has to reach *up* to his plate, not *down* like an adult. Then assume that position yourself. And see how long it is before *you* spill your milk and drop peas on the floor.

In a world where everything's designed to adult scale, the child loses. Do what you can to build your child's self-esteem by helping him not lose quite so often. Take a few easy, reasonable steps to simplify your child's environment.

4—STATE FACTS, DON'T EVALUATE

I think we're all pretty much guilty of poor communication techniques with our children. The trouble is that when they do something we don't like, we *evaluate* our child's behavior, rather than simply stating how their behavior makes us feel.

Showing your child that his behavior has a negative effect on you will do a lot more toward changing it than pointing out what he's done.

When you're upset with your child, don't send you-messages. Send I-messages.

You-messages evaluate, criticize, point out faults and failings. I-messages emphasize feelings and reactions.

Suppose Alicia and Allen are chasing each other around the room. Your first reaction will be to shout at them, "You kids are really being rude. Settle down!" The children will hear what you're saying and make this interpretation: "We're rude kids. We don't care about how Dad feels."

But if you send an I-message, their interpretation will be more accurate, and their self-esteem will be salvaged. You say, "Hey, I'm trying to concentrate, and I can't when it's noisy." This time they don't think they're rotten kids. Instead they'll think that Dad's trying to concentrate.

All that difference comes just from trying to state your feelings instead of trying to lay blame.

5—BE EMPATHETIC, NOT PREACHY

Preston is outside playing with a neighborhood friend. They have a fight, and Preston comes in crying to you. You feel bad, so you try to reassure him. "Carlos doesn't really hate you, son. He was just mad."

Wrong! Try again.

When your child is upset, don't be preachy, giving him reasoning or reassurance. Give him empathy.

There's an important reason for this. When a child comes to you for help, he wants understanding. He wants acknowledgement that you recognize his feelings and that you care about them. If you respond with reasoning or reassurance, he's going to feel that you don't understand him at all. And a child who doesn't feel understood is one with low self-esteem.

Let's try with Preston again. "Carlos hates me!" he shouts. "He said so!"

Sit down by him. "You feel really bad that he said that, don't you?" you say.

"Yes. He always wants things his own way. If I try to do what I want, he gets mad and yells at me."

"That's pretty upsetting, isn't it? It never feels good to have someone yell at you."

Empathy. Preston knows that Carlos doesn't really hate him but he needs you to feel bad with him.

"Well, I'm going back out to play," says Preston. "Carlos and I are building boats."

When you let your child know that you can feel his feelings with him, he feels loved. Cared for. He knows that those feelings are valid, that this person he calls *me* is a valid *self*.

6—DON'T TAKE
OVER FOR HIM

It's Jenny's new job to set the table. The first night Mom helps her, showing her where to put the silverware, the plates, the glasses, the napkins. The next night they do it together, just to make sure Jenny has the right idea. So far, so good.

But on night three Jenny gets to solo. She haphazardly lumps the silverware by the side of each plate. She forgets to put the pepper on the table for her father. She puts the napkins on top of each plate, instead of by the side like her mother taught her.

"Your memory's about as short as a sheep's tail," Mom complains. She stomps over to the table, towering over poor Jenny, and proceeds to set the table right. "There!" Mom says. "That's how it's done." Jenny looks up at her mother, her eyes filled with tears.

I hope you've never done that—but chances are you have!

When you give a job or a responsibility to your child, let him do it in his own way. If he blows it, don't do the job over. That will only serve to undercut his self-esteem.

After all, what's more important: that the table be set right or that your child feel good about himself?

Of course, you can still correct your children when they make a mistake with their assignment. But correct the child, not his work. "Jenny, did you forget where the spoon should go?"

Jenny looks and corrects it herself. This way she learns how to correctly do her task, and at the same time she's able to retain her self-esteem.

If you constantly take over for your children, you're defeating yourself twice. First, you're damaging their delicate egos. And second, you're ensuring that they'll never learn to do the job right by themselves.

7—HELPING IN FRUSTRATION

There are many things that frustrate us about life—and this is especially true for a child. There's so much your child hasn't learned to do yet, but so much that he wants and tries to do.

Frustration is inevitable. It happens to even the most competent of our children, and you can't do anything to prevent it. But you can make a difference in how it affects your child's self-image. Here's how:

When your child is frustrated, help him work through it. By helping him become more competent in that particular area, you're boosting his self-esteem.

Tammy is sitting at the dining room table working on her first-grade homework. Suddenly she crumples up the papers and throws them on the floor. "I'm so stupid! I can't do anything right!" says Tammy.

If her mom just lets it pass, Tammy may leave the experience really believing herself. But there's a much better way. Her mom uncrumples the papers and smoothes them out on the table. "This lettering can be kind of hard, can't it," says her mom, who shows that she understands Tammy's frustration. "Which letters are giving you the most trouble?" she asks.

"All of them!" answers Tammy.

But as they talk together, her mom learns which letters are giving Tammy the most trouble: the ones with descenders like g, p, y. She shows Tammy how to write these letters, refreshing her memory, then watches while Tammy practices.

Helping your child overcome frustrations is no more difficult than simply spending the time to help him become more proficient at the thing that's frustrating him.

8—NEVER WITHHOLD LOVE

Following this instruction is crucial if you want your child to have a healthy self-image.

Children aren't consistent in showing their love to their parents, because they are still immature. A child is just trying to find himself, to learn his place in the world.

But some parents make the mistake of withholding love as a means of punishment. "He's being a brat just to spite me. Well, I'll show him!" To teach their child a lesson, these parents refuse to show affection or even to speak civilly to the child.

The result is a heavy blow to his self-esteem.

If you want to have a child who feels good about himself, remember this: when you need to discipline, do it with love. If that's too much to ask, then do this: after you discipline, immediately renew the bonds of affection with your child.

And never use the withholding of love as an implement with which to train your child.

A scientist who worked with chimps once learned this lesson the hard way. Whenever a chimp wouldn't respond, the scientist grew aloof and punishing. The chimp quickly grew confused, disoriented, unable to perform even the simple tasks that he'd already mastered. The scientist's love and approval had been the rod to which the chimp had clung. When it was removed, the chimp lost the advances he'd made.

Don't make the same mistake with your children!

9—YOUR CHILD'S FRIENDS

Some parents feel they should let their children select their own friends. Certainly this kind of independence is desirable—within limits. The limits are these: you should let your child decide who he wants to play with, but you should help him with general guidelines to make sure that the peer influence he's subjected to is acceptable.

When your child grows older, of course, he'll probably do as he pleases in choosing friends. The time to have influence is before he goes to school.

And here's an important principle: **show an interest in your child's friends**.

If you seem to care about who Billy plays with, Billy will know that yet another aspect of his life matters to you. His self-esteem, ever mirrored from you, will climb.

When Billy brings home a new friend, don't just say, "Wipe your feet!" and no more. Spend a few minutes with the boys, and find out a little bit about his new playmate. Who are his parents? Where does the boy come from? Where does he live? How old is he? What are his favorite toys? What are his favorite foods?

Become friends with your child's friends. Know their names, their attitudes, their fears and joys.

This will take a little time, won't it? And what are the dividends? A child who knows that you like him to be part of your life. A child who is proud to be who he is, because he's obviously a person who has a solid place in his own home.

And when you treat Billy's friends with that kind of regard, they're going to treat *Billy* with more respect. "Gee, Billy, your mom's pretty neat. You have a neat family."

His self-image will be boosted twice.

10—STIMULATE
HIS INTELLECT

Sam enjoys school and does well at it. He likes to read and write—just like his dad.

Becky hates everything about her school. She thinks that her teacher doesn't care about her and that her studies are too hard. About the only redeeming features she can think of are recess and lunch.

It's not hard to guess which child has higher self-esteem. Does Sam feel better about himself because he does well intellectually—or does he do well intellectually because he has self-esteem? The answer to both questions is yes! Your child's self-image is affected by his ability to do well during his six classroom hours nearly every day of his first eighteen years. But if he has a good self-image to begin with, he's able to get a better start at his task.

You can give your child a step in the right direction by stimulating his intellect before he starts school. If you do, he'll have a stronger self-image and also do better at school.

How can you help your child be a Sam and not a Becky? Just a few suggestions:

1. Read to your child from a very early age. Books are available for nearly every level of a child's intellectual development.

2. Let your child see you enjoy reading. This will show him that reading is a desirable activity.

3. When he asks you a question, don't just give a quick answer and then brush him off, especially if he seems genuinely interested in details. Learn the details with him.

4. Take opportunities to show him how exciting learning can be. When you see a caterpillar in your backyard, tell him about the stages of its development. Show him some pictures, then help him watch for the appearance of a cocoon later in the season.

5. Expose your child to adults and children from different

backgrounds. Help him see how wide the world really is.

I could go on with ideas forever, but the best ones will come from your own love of learning. That love, plus a good relationship with your child, can honestly make the difference between his success and failure at school—and his accompanying self-image.

11—USE BUILDING NICKNAMES

"Hey, Fats, get your elbows off the table!"

"Think you can catch it this time, Butterfingers?"

Maybe your child is overweight. Maybe his head is a little pointed on the top, or maybe he's clumsy.

If he's any one of these—or one of a hundred other things—you can be certain he's struggling with his self-esteem. He's different from others in an undesirable way and that difference makes him wonder if he's as valuable a person as those around him.

If you're going to use nicknames with your child, choose a name that will build his self-image. Choose one that will point out a positive aspect of his person.

Building nicknames build a child's self-esteem. Critical, negative nicknames tear it down.

Suppose your son is chubby, but he's also strong for his age. Call him Tarzan, Superman, Atlas, Mr. Strong.

Maybe your daughter honestly has a pointed head, but she also has a very pleasant personality. Call her Happy, Smiles, Joy.

Another daughter is clumsy, but she's also smart. Call her Smarts, Brains, Thinker.

Of course, you have to choose a name that's comfortable for you. And one that really does fit the child.

Whenever you use a nickname, be sure you use it as a term of *endearment*, not of sarcasm. Your tone of voice when you say the name will make all kinds of difference.

12—HAVE PERSONAL SELF-ESTEEM

Some parents try to help their children have high self-esteem when they themselves don't have it. But this won't work.

Your child learns an incredible amount from you. Most of what he learns is from your actions, not your words. If you treat him in a way that will build his self-esteem, but don't do the same for yourself, he'll pick up on the discrepancy. And your effort to build his self-esteem will be weakened.

If you hope to build your child's self-esteem, work from a base of strong self-esteem yourself.

There are two important reasons why this is a sound principle: modeling and gratification.

Modeling. Your child mimics you in subtle ways that you'll never know. He looks at who you are and tries to make himself like you. After all, you're the most important being in his entire universe. If you project a model of low self-esteem, that's the model he'll use in his own self-development.

Gratification. Some parents who have low self-esteem use their children's accomplishments as boosters. Since they've never developed their own self-esteem, these parents get their feelings of worth almost entirely from their children. In other words, their desires for high self-esteem and high accomplishment in their children are primarily selfish. The result is unfortunate—the child will usually "let the parent down," and both will end up feeling of less worth as persons.

How do you build your own self-esteem? For starters, you can use the principles in this book. My bet is that you've been *treating yourself* in many of the negative ways this book warns against. If you want your child to have high self-esteem, you need to turn the tables and make the effort to reverse the trend in your own life. Find your strengths and let yourself have successful experiences in those areas. Find your areas of worth and capitalize on them. *Use this book on yourself.*

13—BE POLITE

Children can be utter pests. They're underfoot at the worst times. They're not around when you need them. They argue and disobey.

The temptation is to fight fire with fire. If Zachary yells at you, you yell back. If he starts to argue, you argue too.

But when we take this approach, we forget that kids are people too. For example, I remember my dad bitterly reprimanding me and then politely answering a telephone call, giving a stranger on the phone more consideration than me.

Treating your children politely shows them that they're important as people, that they're worth at least as much respect as anyone else in your life.

For example: "Ruth, will you please clear the dishes off the table?"

"Ralph, it's time to get ready for bed. Please run upstairs."

"Henry, thanks for taking the trash out. That really helped me."

"Excuse me, Jill. I didn't mean to bump into you."

These words are magic in more ways than one. They'll help things run more smoothly. They'll help your children be more cooperative and polite. But, even more importantly, the magic words and acts of politeness will help your child see that you *respect* him and will gradually instill a feeling of *self*-respect in your child. And self-respect is only one step removed from self-esteem.

Politeness is one small thing you can do for your child that will pay off in big dividends throughout his entire life.

14—MAKE SURE THAT FAMILY RULES ARE UNDERSTOOD

Nothing is more frustrating than to break a rule that you never knew existed. I remember a bad experience I had when I was a college student. The professor gave us a crucial assignment and stressed that the final product was to be packaged in a certain way. Somehow I misunderstood and turned my assignment in wrong. The quality of my work was good, but I had done the wrong work.

That happens all the time with our children. Children basically desire to please their elders, and if they know what's *really* expected, they'll usually do their best to deliver. The problems arise when the family rules are not clearly defined.

Then, when they perform in good faith, they soon discover that they've missed the boat, and that instead of pleasing you, they've disappointed you. Imagine what that does to their self-esteem:

"I can't do anything right!"

"Everybody else can please Mom and Dad. Not me!"

"I guess I'm just not worth much."

How can you make sure that your family rules are clearly understood by everyone in the family? The first step is to get each child involved in discussing the rules.

The second step is to have the child restate those rules in his own language. If he can verbalize them in his own way, you've probably successfully communicated them.

Third, institute the rules immediately—but have an unannounced grace period in which you work out any misunderstandings.

These three steps will help assure that every member of your family has a clear understanding of what's expected.

This clear understanding of the family's rules is vital in the effort of building your child's self-esteem.

15—GIVE APPROVAL

You can't give your child too much approval, unless you're condoning things that he's doing wrong. You're the center of his universe, and he needs to know that he *fits*, that he's an acceptable part of *your* world.

The more approval your child receives from you, the better he'll feel about himself.

If your child somehow feels that you don't approve of him as a person, he'll make repeated attempts to gain that approval. You'll *dis*approve of many of those attempts—but your child doesn't know that until he tries. And of course he'll fumble; he isn't even aware of exactly what it is he's after. He just knows there's a hole in his feelings about himself.

Rob whined around the house, getting into things until he nearly drove his mom nuts. Finally her patience crumbled. "Knock it off, Robert," she shouted. "Every day it's the same!" Of course, this didn't help matters.

Rob's behavior grew more extreme, as he frantically sought his mother's approval.

When Rob's mother learned that she needed to show approval for his *positive* actions, no matter what his negative actions were, his behavior improved. Why? She was showing Rob that he mattered, that he was a valuable person in her life.

How do you show approval? There are many ways, both subtle and overt. Every child understands a smile, a pat, a hug, a moment of your directed attention. Even an infant will respond to the warmth of your voice, and children ages two and up will understand your expressions of praise and appreciation. Most important of all, *approval is an attitude*. If you honestly do approve of your child as a person, even if you don't like all of his actions, he'll perceive your basic attitude and feel good about himself.

16—HAVE "SELF-ESTEEM" TALKS TOGETHER

It makes you feel good when someone you love talks intimately with you—when they share how they really feel and listen to you. That's probably the best part of a good talk: when the other person lets *you* talk, when they obviously care how you feel.

It's no different for a child. When you let them talk to you, they feel closer to you. They feel better about themselves.

Spend time talking with your child, and he'll feel good twice: once because you're spending time with him, and once because you're talking about him.

Here are a few ideas you can use to start a good self-esteem talk with your child:

Have him tell you "Things I'm good at."

Play this game: "If I were an animal, I'd be _____, because it's good at _____."

Have her tell you "Things I'm proud of."

Have him tell you "Things I did well today."

Ask her to explore her feelings and tell "How I feel right now."

Ask him to tell you "Things I like or don't like about my body."

Have her explain "Something I did for someone else today."

Have him tell what you (the parent) did that made him feel good today.

Tell her what she did that made you feel good today.

Tell him what it felt like when he was born. Tell him about how things were when he was little.

Have him tell you about good things he remembers from when he was younger.

17—DO
BUILDING ACTIVITIES

Sometimes a parent can spend some high-quality time specifically building his child's self-esteem. By participating together in self-esteem building activities, you'll strengthen your child in two ways:

1. By showing your child he's special, that you enjoy being with just him.

2. By building him through the activity itself.

Spend time in special activities with your child, and you'll build his self-esteem.

Here are a few things you can do together:

Have your child draw "a picture of me" or have him put together a collage from magazine scraps.

Spend some time with your child choosing some symbols of successes he's experienced (a paper he got a good grade on at school, a trophy from a pinewood derby, a torn pair of pants that demonstrates how he learned to ride a bike, or a picture of him and Dad with his first fish). Use these symbols to decorate his room.

Have a day where you celebrate "Child for a Day!" Spend the whole day making your child know how much you love and appreciate her. Let her choose the menus for each meal, go on a special outing with her, give her some special but inexpensive gifts. This is especially effective if you have more than one child.

Take your child's fingerprints and hang them on your wall.

Get a large sheet of butcher paper or newsprint, have your child lie down on it, and trace around his body. Then let your child color in his clothing and features. Hang it on his wall.

Set goals together, and put them on a chart. Hang the chart in an obvious place and review and update it periodically. The goals should be things that your child really wants to accomplish, not things *you* want her to do.

Make a family tree, showing where you and your child and other family members fit. Include grandparents and great-grandparents.

18—TEACH PATIENCE

Mother and Father were talking at the dinner table, trying to resolve a financial problem. It wasn't the best time and place to try to solve that kind of problem, and Emmy interrupted them.

"Mommy," she said, impatiently.

"Just a minute, Emmy."

"Mommy."

"I'll talk to you in a minute, Emmy. I'm trying to talk to your father."

"*Mommy!*"

Emmy kept after it until she had totally disrupted her parents' conversation, made her mother mad at her, and ruined the supper for everyone—all because she lacked the virtue of patience.

Patience is like any other kind of self-mastery: when a child learns it, he gets two benefits. First, he wins the approval of his parents, and approval leads to higher self-esteem. Second, he wins the approval of himself, meaning he feels better about the kind of person he is. And self-approval leads to higher self-esteem.

To raise your children's self-esteem, teach them to be patient. Since we all live in an uncooperative world, it will make the rest of their lives go better.

When your child is impatient with you, don't give in to her demands—unless your own preoccupation isn't warranted anyway. If you can't attend to your child right away, tell her exactly how soon you can talk to her, then stick to it.

Help your child learn that patience is a "skill" by playing a "patience game." Start by challenging the child to be completely quiet for one minute and time him with the kitchen timer. As he succeeds, he'll grow more self-confident. Then raise the time to two minutes—then five, then ten. Eventually the child will see that he *can* be patient, and as he's more and more successful, his self-esteem will rise.

19—TEACH RESPONSIBILITY

Nan knew that she was supposed to do her chores but she chose instead to play with her dolls until suppertime. When she came down the stairs, hungry, she expected to find the food all ready and waiting. But the table was unset—it was Nan's job, and no one had done it for her.

Nan's mom knew that when you give a child responsibility, you should never take it back. If your child's irresponsibility causes everyone else to suffer, make sure they know about it. But don't nag, threaten, or bribe. Simply be firm and unmoving: "It's your job, and you're responsible for it. If you can't set the table, we'll all just have to wait until you do."

(Of course, everyone doesn't have to suffer just because of Nan. Feed everyone snacks to tide them over until Nan does her job. Nan, of course, doesn't get any such snacks.)

Mike started to do his homework, but he was being distracted by the TV and his brothers playing in the next room. Finally, it was bedtime—and the homework still wasn't done. Mom put him to bed anyway, despite his protests that he'd get a bad grade.

The next night Mom tried to make it easier on Mike. She helped him set up a desk in his room, so he wouldn't have so many distractions. He still had difficulty concentrating, and Mom found that she had to use supportive methods. She promised to read him a story if he finished his homework before bedtime. Another night she told him he'd get to stay up an extra half hour if he finished his homework by bedtime.

Soon Mike was consistently doing his homework on his own. His mom's support paid off.

Being responsible covers the gamut of life—from doing homework to doing chores to remembering not to splash water when taking a bath. The keys to teaching responsibility are simple: just give praise, give support, and be persistent. Make sure your child knows what's expected. Make sure your expectations are realistic.

As your child learns to be more responsible, he'll find his self-image growing more and more in positive ways. He'll see that he's a valuable person who can be trusted, and he'll value himself more and more because of it.

20—ENCOURAGE PERSEVERANCE

Teddy was trying to put together a simple puzzle, but the pieces wouldn't fit. He turned them every-which-way, and he tried all kinds of combinations. No matter what he did, it wouldn't work.

But he didn't give up. He kept after it, trying one piece after another, and gradually he made progress.

Other days he might have given up in defeat. But not today because his dad encouraged him:

"Teddy, I'm glad that you're working so well on that puzzle. It's hard for you, but you're not giving up. You just keep trying."

Parents should encourage perseverance in their children. Perseverance is a quality that builds self-esteem. The more a child perseveres, the more success she'll achieve. And success leads directly to heightened self-esteem.

When a child gives in to discouragement or fatigue, she suffers a loss of self-respect. Sometimes it's best to leave a job and return to it later, but it can be damaging to anyone to start a job and then give up on it indefinitely.

There are a lot of areas in which perseverance is important:
chores
schoolwork
competitive play
personal projects
learning a new skill.

When your child wants to give up, encourage him to persevere. It's more than a matter of getting something done; it's a matter of self-image. Does your child view himself as a quitter? Then he'll find it easier and easier to quit, all the while finding himself less valuable as a person.

Praise your child when she continues at something even though it's somewhat difficult. Set a good example by being persevering yourself. Let her know it's better to get help on a hard project than to give up.

21—PUT YOUR MARRIAGE FIRST

Some parents have their primary relationship with their *children*. They spend most of their time with the children. They seek pleasure and fulfillment from the children.

In these cases the spouse has a secondary place. The promises "to have, to hold, to love, and to cherish" get lost in the shuffle—suddenly it's the children that this parent is having, holding, loving, and cherishing.

Logically, it would seem that smothering a child with love would help him to have more self-esteem—after all, this shows how important he is to you, right? Wrong! It shows how important his success and achievement and love are to you. And there's a world of difference between the two. In the first, the emphasis is on *him*. In the second, it's on *you*.

The solution is to put first things first again. Parents need to have their primary relationship with each other. If you care for your children at the expense of your spouse, everyone suffers—you, your spouse, and your children.

Children need to be free of that kind of heavy bond. Eventually they will leave the nest, and if your primary relationship is with your spouse, they'll have the self-esteem to make it on their own. And, if your spouse has been first in your life, you'll be able to adjust easily to the "empty nest" years.

Have your primary relationship with your spouse. Let your children be vitally important in your life, but remember that your spouse comes first. This will strengthen the family unit and will help your children's self-esteem at the same time.

In this kind of an environment, the children won't have to succeed *for the parent*; they can succeed for themselves.

22—LET YOUR CHILD BE SELF-RELIANT

A child will gradually, step-by-step, declare his independence from his parents in order to be self-reliant.

Self-reliance in a child is sometimes hard to accept, but it should not only be accepted, it should also be encouraged.

If you try to prevent your child's natural tendency to become self-reliant, you'll have a child who is too dependent on you. The result may be a child who isn't sure he can function on his own, a child who doubts his competence and capability in dealing with life, a child who has low self-esteem.

Encourage your child to be self-reliant, and you'll build that self-esteem. You'll help her gradually become more and more successful in life—on her own.

There are two basic things you can do to encourage self-reliance. The first is to let your child try things himself, even if he fails time and again. As long as he's willing to try a new thing, let him. And praise his efforts.

For example, you can say, "Gregory, I'm glad you're trying to tie your shoes by yourself. That's an important thing to know how to do."

The second way to encourage self-reliance is to let your child function on his own once he learns a new skill. Even if he tries to revert back to dependence (and this can be allowed in small doses, especially when the child has had a traumatic day), you should encourage him to do the task on his own:

"Gregory, you've learned to tie your shoes by yourself. That's exciting, isn't it? It's good to know how to do things for yourself. I know you want me to help you tie them today, but you should tie them yourself. When you're done, come down to the kitchen and I'll sing some songs to you while I wash the dishes."

23—REFUSE
TO BE MANIPULATED

"Mommy, I want a snack," Carol whines. Mommy says no.

"Please, Mommy. Just a little one," asks Carol. "No," says her mom again.

Carol starts to whine more and more loudly: "I'm *so* hungry." "No," says her mom for the third time.

For a solid ten minutes, Mommy refuses Carol's demand, but finally she gives in. "Oh, all right, you can have your darn snack," she says.

Mommy doesn't know it, but Carol has just followed a script word for word. Carol knew that Mommy would say "No." But she knew that if she kept after Mommy, before long she would give in and let her have what she wanted.

Carol has *manipulated* Mommy into getting her the snack. And that's unfortunate, because Carol's hunger was appeased for a while, but her self-esteem was weakened. When her mother gave in, she was saying, in effect:

"My comfort is more important than your safety."

Carol's mom had established a rule. She felt she had strong reasons for the rule, but when the going got tough, she gave in and didn't stick to her rule. "I wanted to protect you," she says through her actions, "but you're bothering me so much that that's no longer important. I'll give in to you to protect myself."

It's a complicated thing, an issue that involves many different facets of the human personality. But in the end the child loses his feelings of security and value in the home.

Never give in to your child's manipulating. She'll lose her feelings of self-esteem, even if only a small measure. And the next time she'll manipulate even more.

Children are masters of manipulation. They'll pout, whine, cry, scream, fight, and act cute to get you to break your rules. But don't give in to them. They'll respect you—and themselves—more if you don't. And, if you're consistent, pretty soon they'll stop trying.

If you're going to be firm against manipulating tactics, be sure that you have good reasons for your rules. Maybe Carol's mother didn't have a good reason for not letting Carol have a snack—in which case she should let her have one in the first place.

Have a good reason for the rules you set, and then stick to them. If you do, everyone will feel better.

24—HAVE CLEAR AREAS OF RESPONSIBILITY

In the Martin home there's a chart on the refrigerator that outlines every family member's chores. The responsibilities rotate, so one week, for example, a child takes out the garbage and the next week she sets the table. Of course, all the chores depend on the age of each child.

The chart lists the following responsibilities:

> set and clear the table
> wash the dishes
> dry the dishes and put them away
> dump all the trash baskets into the garbage can outside
> put the garbage on the street on Tuesday night
> vacuum the family room and living room.

Everyone knows what they're supposed to do and when they're supposed to do it. It's a great system. The work gets done, usually with a minimum of reminders. Everyone in the family knows that the workload is shared pretty much equally. The system helps all family members feel that they're an important part of the family, and it gives each one a regular success experience.

Success experiences lead to self-esteem. The more a child is able to do things well, the better he'll feel about himself. Because the family has clear areas of responsibility, every family member feels good about himself as a person.

The Martin family's system is custom-made, and it probably wouldn't work for every family. But they've found an important key to building self-esteem: have clear areas of responsibility in the family.

25—INVOLVE THE CHILD
IN SETTING LIMITS

Motivational experts have found that a person obeys rules much more readily when he's had a hand in setting them, and this applies to children too.

Children may be smaller, less verbally efficient, weaker, and less mature, but they have the same feelings as adults. When they are able to help set the limits they have to live by, they're more likely to obey them. They feel better about the family and their relationship with it. They feel better about themselves.

Involving your child in setting his limits will build his self-esteem. It will show him he's important to the family. And since he'll obey the limits more, he'll have more success, which builds self-esteem even further.

Setting limits can occur both formally and informally. When you do it formally, you sit down together expressly for the purpose of making the rules:

"I don't like you to stay so long over at your friend's house. I asked you to come back after an hour and you didn't come. I know you don't know what time it is, but I don't want to come chasing after you. What do you think we can do?"

When you set limits informally, you do it on the spot, right when the problem occurs:

"I said you could play outside if you'd watch Billy—and you let him wander out into the street. What should we do so you can have fun and still help take care of Billy?"

Having your child help you to set her own limits will get her more and more involved in problem solving, which will further expand her world and will boost her self-esteem even more. Your household will run smoother; your family will be happier; and your child will grow up feeling more capable and competent.

26—DON'T REQUIRE BLIND OBEDIENCE

"Get your elbows off the table," says Mom. "Why?" asks Jimmy. "Because I said so," answers Mom.

"Stop making so much racket," says Dad. "Why?" asks Amy. "Because I don't like it," answers Dad.

"You'd better have your room picked up in five minutes," says Sue's mother. "Why?" she asks. "Because you'd better, that's why!" says her mom.

Parents who require blind obedience of their children are making a mistake, because they may get the obedience they seek, but

they're not teaching their children the *why* of things;

they're not respecting their children as individuals with feelings and needs;

they're being dictators rather than benevolent leaders;

they're teaching their children to be dependent upon orders, rather than to learn to think for themselves.

The child who learns to obey blindly doesn't respect himself. He has come to view himself as an appendage to his parents, a tool to do what they order.

Some children may rebel, and these children lose their sense of belonging in the family. They lose some of their attachment to their parents, and in this process, they also lose their self-respect.

Don't require blind obedience of your children. Give them reasons for the things you ask them to do. This will help them feel important; it will boost their self-esteem.

For example: "Get your elbows off the table, please," says Mom. "Why?" asks Jimmy. "Because it's more polite when you're eating to leave your elbows off the table," replies Mom. "That's a part of good table manners. People will enjoy eating with you more if you have good manners."

"Please stop making so much racket," says Dad. "Why?" asks Amy. "Because I've had a hard day, and now I have a headache," answers Dad. "I get nervous and feel worse when there's a lot of noise around. I'm feeling more and more tense, and I'm afraid I'll really get mad and yell at you if you don't quiet down. I don't want to do that, especially since you're not the cause of my problems. Maybe it would work if you went into another room, and we can be together and have some fun later."

"You'd better have your room picked up in five minutes," says Sue's mother. "Why?" asks Sue. "Because in five minutes I'm going to take you to school, and I don't like having a dirty house all day," replies her mom. "It's not fair for me to have to clean up your mess. If you pitch right in and work on it, you can have it cleaned up quickly."

27—BE CONSISTENT

On Thursday Dennis splashed water all over the bathroom floor as he brushed his teeth. His mother was furious, and she spanked him.

On Friday Dennis splashed water all over the bathroom again, but his mother was in a good mood. She sent him off to play while she cleaned up the mess.

Dennis knew that he shouldn't splash water all over the bathroom, but his mother was so inconsistent that he never knew what to expect when he broke the rule. He never knew where he stood with her.

Children need consistency in the enforcement of rules. This gives them security and a sense of belonging. It reinforces their feelings of worth and self-esteem.

Animal trainers use the rule of consistency. If they want an animal, say a lion, to learn a particular trick, they go through the same routine over and over, never varying, until the lion learns the trick.

The trainer's consistency is valuable for two reasons: first, it helps the lion know exactly what is wanted. The lion always knows where he stands and where the trainer stands. Second, the lion learns to respect the trainer. The trainer doesn't back down, and he doesn't quit. He keeps after the lion, *consistently*, until he reaches his goal.

The same rule of consistency applies across nature. If you want your child to feel important, make sure that he understands the rules and then enforce them consistently.

Part of consistency comes from the unity of the parents. If one parent requires one thing and another parent requires something else, the child will be uncertain about herself. She'll be unsure how she can find success with both parents. And that success, of course, is vital to her feelings of self-worth.

Certainly there are extenuating circumstances that may call for the review of a rule in a particular instance. But if a parent chooses to vary from the rule, he should explain to the child what he's doing and why. This will help the child know how she fits into the family organization and will help her feel an important part of it.

28—BE COMPROMISING

You can also build your children's self-esteem by being willing to compromise, setting rules clearly *but flexibly*—never worrying about your own weakness but considering only what's best for your child, your family, your relationship.

This is the greatest kind of strength there is.

Compromise and flexibility cause self-esteem to flourish.

Every rule has its exception. You may unequivocally state that your children *must* be home by five o'clock so you can serve dinner. And that may be a perfectly good rule in your household. But when your daughter wants to take a dance class that doesn't end until 5:30, you make an exception.

The same kind of exception can be applied equally well to more important, more complex rules. Make compromises. For example, your son wants to skip his chores tonight, because he has too much homework. You analyze the situation and agree with him—you change the rule for the evening.

You'll find many times during a single week when you need to be flexible. Flexibility and compromise are the only rules that should never be changed! If you observe these rules strictly, you'll be telling your child that *he* is more important than the rules.

To paraphrase the Bible, "Children were not made for the benefit of rules; rules were made for the benefit of children!"

29—SET CLEAR RULES

When I was younger, I remember complaining that my mother was too strict: "Barry's mom lets him stay out late; why can't I? Tom's dad let *him* buy a car—why can't I have one?"

My mother's answer was an enigma to me: "I set these rules so you'll know I love you."

That was hard for me to understand. Didn't Barry and Tom feel loved? Yes. And they had their late nights and cars to enjoy.

What I didn't realize was that Barry and Tom had other limits. They had rules of their own that helped them feel loved. Those rules helped them feel important too.

My mom was right. And now I understand:

Set clear rules for your children, and you'll build their self-esteem.

Rules serve a double purpose when it comes to esteem. First, they tell the child that you care about him. That means you're interested in his welfare. You won't let him do just anything that comes into his mind, because you don't want him to get hurt physically or emotionally. You want him to grow sound and strong, because you care a great deal. You have esteem for your child; and this, of course, leads to *self*-esteem.

Second, rules tell a child where she stands. They erect a fence around her, which gives a sense of security. And it tells her exactly what she must do to find success in your home. As she obeys the rules, the success comes automatically—and success automatically leads to greater self-esteem.

You hold your child in high enough regard to set high standards for him. In return, he gradually begins to hold himself in high regard.

30—ALLOW YOUR CHILD
TO EXPRESS HIMSELF

The family is sitting at the dinner table. While they eat, Dad discusses the family vacation. "Why don't we go to the beach?" Dad says. "It would be fun to build sand castles and swim in the ocean."

"I hate the beach," says Kim. "The sand is dirty, and there are flies. The ocean is too cold to swim in. Sand castles are *dumb*."

"That's enough out of you, young lady," her mom says. "If you can't think of anything nice to say, you can just keep quiet."

As you can tell, families like this do a lot to encourage discussion among their children!

The trouble is that opinions are being expressed—and invited. Kim has opinions herself, and they're perfectly valid to her, so she expresses them. But her parents only want to hear things that rubber-stamp what they've previously decided.

This is a mistake. Children should be allowed to express themselves openly, without fear of reprisal. They don't need to be unfeeling about others (like Mom and Dad were in the instance above), but they can tell how they *feel*.

Forcing your child to stifle her feelings and opinions tears down her self-image. Allowing and encouraging her to express herself, even though you may disagree with what she says, builds her self-image.

When your child expresses negative feelings, try to find out why he feels that way.

For example, Mom asks: "Why, Kim, when we went to the beach last time you seemed to have a really good time. Why do you have bad feelings about it now?"

To acknowledge someone else's feelings, even if we don't understand them or agree with them, opens the opportunity for a dialogue. It builds bonds, bringing the two people closer together. Greater understanding is reached, the relationship is strengthened, and the parent and the child both feel better.

31—NEVER RIDICULE

"Hey, everybody look at Rosemary! She looks like a *cow* with her tongue stuck out that way!"

"You smell like a pig. Why don't you ever take a bath?"

I suppose parents who say these kinds of things have good motives. Their intent isn't to ridicule *per se*; it's not simply to make their child feel like a fool. Instead they're trying to shock and shame the child into changing his ways.

Unfortunately, this kind of ploy never works. Instead it shocks and shames the child into believing his parent. He doesn't change; he only gets worse and worse.

Ridicule is effective only in destroying self-esteem. It tears the child down without building him up again. It makes the child believe that you think he's a slob or a fool.

Never use ridicule in dealing with your children. It hurts without helping.

The same applies to *sarcasm*. It hurts without helping:

"You were so fast in doing the dishes there that I thought my head would spin!"

"I can tell from that remark that you really *are* smart!"

The key is to respect your child's dignity as a person. That's the **building** approach. Respect by others leads to self-respect.

Everyone has self-dignity, but if it isn't honored by others, a person soon loses it. On the other hand, if you recognize that your child is a person with feelings and needs, you'll treat her with dignity. This will build her self-respect, and she'll be more willing to respond to the things you'd like her to do.

32—BE KIND

Everyone needs kindness and consideration. Marriages break up over sex and money disagreements, but it's not the disagreements that cause the problem. It's the lack of kindness and consideration during those disagreements. It's possible to have differences of opinion and still be respectful of the other person and his views.

This is no less so with a child. She needs kindness and consideration in large doses. When she doesn't get them, she tends to become defensive—and often will counterattack!

Why? Because she feels her very value as a person threatened, usually in ways she doesn't understand. Her only viable reactions are to withdraw (reinforcing her self-judgment) or to fight back (weakening the bond of respect between parent and child).

Kind and considerate treatment lead to great self-esteem. It shows the child that she's worth the "trouble" to make an effort, even when things get tense. The key word, of course, is "worth."

Rudeness may get the job done, but it certainly doesn't build any feelings of self-respect in a child:

"Shut that door!"

"Why don't you grow up!"

But kindness and consideration do. Perhaps it would help to try to feel a little empathy for your child. What is he feeling now? Why does he feel it? How can I help? What's the best way to treat him now?

Children won't always give kindness and consideration back. They're immature; they're still learning how to handle their emotions and their bodies. It's too much to expect that they'll always behave as adults.

But is that too much to expect of us adults?

33—REGULARLY GIVE PRAISE AND EXPRESS APPRECIATION

"I sure appreciate the way you set the table," says Mom.

"I'm glad you got such good grades on your report card," says Sally's dad.

"I'm proud of how well you spoke your lines in the play," says Johnny's mother. " I noticed everyone enjoyed the part you played—and I probably enjoyed it most of all."

Regular expressions of praise and appreciation do much to build a child's self-esteem. It helps him see what he's done that's right. It helps reinforce his feeling that he's an important person.

It's not difficult to express these kinds of feelings. Parents simply need to watch for opportunities to share positive feelings with their children—and then to share them in a positive way.

Every child does *something* good. Perhaps he's pleasant in the morning when everyone else is grumbly. Maybe he makes his bed; or brushes his teeth without trouble; or plays nicely with friends; or takes good care of his pet; or keeps his room picked up; or gives you hugs when you need them most; or has a warm smile; or learns quickly; or has a good imagination; or is a good athlete; or helps his little brother. Whatever your child's strong point, whatever he does right, take that opportunity to praise him, to express appreciation.

What is the best way to give praise and appreciation? It *does* matter how you say it. When you're praising your child, always do it from your point of view—and tell how you feel. Be specific about what she has done: "I'm sure happy about how you helped Rob with his chores. You showed him a good way to get them done quickly; he seemed really glad."

These kinds of expressions, given regularly, help build your child's opinion of herself. When you give praise and express appreciation, she feels that she is capable of doing worthwhile things. And, by association, she feels that she is a worthwhile person.

34—RESPECT FEELINGS

Child: "I hate spinach!"

Parent: "No, you don't. Spinach is good for you."

Child: "I don't like Gramps to hold me. He hurts me!"

Parent: "That's not true. Gramps loves you very much."

Child: "I'm sad because you ran over my toy."

Parent: "Oh, that was a broken old thing anyway."

When you tell your child that his feelings or perceptions aren't valid, you tell him that he's a person who's unable to make good judgments. You tell him that his feelings don't count, that they don't matter.

Respect the feelings of your child, and you'll build her self-esteem. She'll see that you care about who she really is—and she'll feel that she has worth to you.

As you respect your child's feelings, he'll come to know that every feeling in the world is valid. When you feel anger, you don't deny that feeling. You own up to it. When you feel frustration, you acknowledge it. When you feel joy, you act joyful. That doesn't mean that a child (or you, for that matter) should be allowed to act out his feelings at will. Certainly our expressions of feeling must be schooled and disciplined.

But never, never deny the feeling. For example:

Parent: "Does the spinach taste funny to you? Why don't you take just a couple of bites then—you don't have to eat the rest."

Parent: "Gramps has arthritis, so it's hard for him to be careful. But I'll ask him to try harder."

Parent: "That toy *was* a lot of fun to play with, wasn't it?"

The child's feelings may be different from yours, but who's to say which perceptions are more valid? All feelings are real, and they should be treated with respect. This will help your child feel that you respect *him* more. Then his *self*-respect will climb.

35—AVOID
POWER STRUGGLES

There are lots of things wrong with power struggles. They're ineffective in getting things done. They create bad feelings in the home. They weaken the parents' natural position of authority, and they make a child feel less valuable than he really is.

Avoid power struggles as you make the effort to build your child's self-esteem. Such struggles place an emphasis on power, instead of human feelings, and your child will feel devalued in the process.

Consider the dynamics of the power struggle. It's like the unstoppable force hitting the immovable rock—neither win, and both are damaged. In the power struggle you want your child to do something he doesn't want to do, and there's no way you can get him to do it without making him lose face and a feeling of self-worth. Or maybe he wants to do something that you absolutely forbid. The result is the same.

For example: Bert came to the table with dirty hands. "Go wash your hands," his father says firmly.

"I don't want to," Bert responds. "I'm hungry."

Bert's father saw a problem developing, and he wanted to nip it in the bud. "I said go wash your hands," he says. "Now go do it!"

Bert reached for the potatoes. "No," he says.

Now Dad's teeth are clenched. *"Get up there and wash your hands!"* he yells.

It's the classic power struggle. And there are only two ways out: Dad can back down and show Bert that (1) Dad sometimes makes orders he doesn't intend to follow through on, (2) Dad is treating Bert as an object whose purpose is to obey orders, and (3) Bert's power is greater than Dad's. All destructive results.

The second way out is for Bert to back down and feel that (1) he's not as important in the family as Dad, and (2) as a person he's not very valuable, since he can be manipulated by power.

The answer, of course, is to avoid power struggles in the first place. Cooperate together to come to reasonable solutions. The home may not be a democracy, but it should be a place of cooperation. A cooperative atmosphere is vital for building a child's self-esteem.

36—AVOID FAVORITISM

If you have two or more children, it's often hard to be equally fair to all of them. Some days you'll just feel more loving to one than to another. That's probably unavoidable. The problem arises when you consistently favor one child over another.

Having a favorite is destructive in two ways. First, the child who is not favored gradually (or quickly) loses his self-esteem. He sees he's not as important to you as his brother or sister is. Second, the child who is the favorite sees the discrepancy, and he suffers from acute *false* esteem. He begins to base his feelings of worth on comparison rather than on real value.

Build your children's self-esteem by loving them all equally, at least as much as possible. Have no favorites; spread your affection and attention among all your children.

You probably saw favoritism in the classroom when you were growing up. One student is singled out above all the others as the model the teacher would like everyone to follow. Everyone dislikes that student and calls her the teacher's pet.

Probably that student *was* a good model. He or she undoubtedly did good work and was notably well behaved. But all of the other students were good models also—it's just that their strengths may be in other areas.

Don't choose a parent's pet. It will cause unnecessary strife in your home. You'll raise a child with misplaced feelings of worth, and, to make things worse, your other children may learn to hate and torment the one who is in favor.

Don't make comparisons among your children. Each is an individual with her own skills and strengths.

Don't consistently spend extra time with the model child—it's the others who need time more.

Don't give the most affection to the one who's most affectionate back. Teach all your children you love them; teach each one that she's important to you.

37—SET REASONABLE EXPECTATIONS

Erin spills her milk all over the breakfast table. Dad yells, "You spill your milk *every meal*! Get up to your room!"

Kelvin won't sit still in church, and he talks so loud that he's bothering everyone around him. His mother takes him outside and spanks him.

Rose comes home with all Cs on her report card—again. "You can't watch any more TV until you get those grades up," her parents tell her.

The parents in these three examples all have one thing in common: they have unreasonable expectations for their children. Erin is at the clumsy age; she *can't* be more careful. Kelvin is too young to remember to whisper. He can't understand why it's necessary anyway. Rose is intellectually immature for her age; she tries hard, but average is all she can muster in school.

These unreasonable expectations are destructive. They cause the child to repeatedly experience failure in life. His self-image suffers as a result.

Every parent should regularly review the expectations he has for his children. If your child seems to be failing in something *you* think she should be able to do, it may be that you are expecting too much.

A few questions are in order:

Why do I think my child should be able to do this?

Why is it important to me?

Have I set this expectation because I want to be proud and fulfilled, or because it's best for the child?

Is my child mature enough to meet this expectation?

Are my expectations high enough to provide my child a challenge but low enough to be achievable by my child?

Do I treat the child as though the expectation were more important than he is?

How can I best set expectations to build my child's self-esteem and to enable her to have regular success experiences?

38—SUPPORT YOUR CHILD'S EXPANDING HORIZONS

Every child inevitably grows older! That statement is more profound than it may at first appear, because as a child grows up, his needs for support change. When your child's world expands, you'll find that she needs support in her new activities and the new aspects of her life.

For example: Wendy has a baseball game this Thursday. "Sorry, Wendy," her folks say. "We just can't make it." Wendy feels crushed. She thinks that what she's doing isn't important to her parents.

Andrea receives a phone call from a friend, but she's not there to take it. Her dad takes a message and puts it up on the family's message board. When Andrea comes home, she sees the message on the board. "Gee, it's sure nice Dad cares enough to take my messages," she thinks.

Ron is in his room writing some personal thoughts in his diary. His door is closed, but his mother barges in without knocking. "Hey, what are you writing there, Ron?" she asks. "Let me take a look." Ron pulls back, withdraws. "Doesn't Mom know that this is *private*?" he thinks.

Children of all ages are worthy of the same considerations their parents expect. Suppose you were doing something important to you; you'd want your family members there to root for you, to cheer in victory and to commiserate in defeat.

Suppose you received a telephone call when you weren't home; you'd expect someone to take a message.

Suppose you were doing something privately in your room, with your door shut; you'd expect a knock on the door before someone else came in and a minimum of nosiness when they did come in.

As children grow, they learn the common courtesies of daily living. They know you expect to receive them.

If you give those courtesies to your children, you build their self-image. You make them feel important.

39—CHILD-PROOF YOUR HOME

Everyone has heard of child-proofing a home. But what in the world does this have to do with a child's self-esteem?

When a home is *not* child-proofed, the child constantly meets with failure. He explores and is reprimanded. He touches something, and his hand is slapped. He plays in the wrong place, and he's spanked and sent to his room.

That child is living with two destructive things: *frustration* and *negativism*. Neither contributes to a healthy self-esteem.

To help your child feel good about herself and her development, child-proof her environment.

Barbara pulls all the books off her mom's shelf. "Don't do that!" Mother says sharply.

Danny's mother lets him play with the pots and pans in the kitchen. When Mother passes him while she's doing her work, she smiles. "Those toys are fun, aren't they," she says.

Barbara opens the basement door and toddles down the stairs. Soon her mom notices she's missing and grows increasingly frantic when she can't find her. Then she sees the basement door open a crack. Barbara gets a spanking when Mother reaches her. "You know you're not supposed to be down here," she says.

Danny's basement door is locked. He wanders aimlessly for a few minutes and then goes to his older sister's room to play with the toys he can reach. Those are the ones his mom and sister let him play with.

Which child is getting frequent boosts to his self-esteem? Which is constantly being torn down? The answer, of course, is obvious. And the whole difference lies in child-proofing the home.

40—SET THE RIGHT STAGE

It's been a hard day at the office. Pressures, tensions, unreasonable demands. Both Mom and Dad enjoy the chance to just relax with their children and to play with them before bedtime.

Soon Dad is rolling on the floor with Jerry, their oldest, wrestling and tickling. Jerry writhes and giggles. "It's so much fun to be with Dad!" he thinks.

They play for a few minutes, then Dad playfully swats Jerry on the rump: "Okay, sport, that's it. Time to get to bed."

"Okay, Dad." Jerry gropes for one more tickle, hoping to get one in return.

Dad pushes him away. "Come on. Up to bed."

Jerry reluctantly climbs the stairs. But soon he's back down again. "Mom, come and tuck me in." She tucks him in.

Then he's down again. "Dad, I need a drink."

And again. "I'm scared."

Again. "I can't go to sleep."

After an hour and a half, they finally get Jerry to bed. After a firm spanking, a firm talking to, and a firm marching up the stairs with a parent's hand firmly around his arm—three times each.

"I can't understand it," Dad says when Jerry's finally asleep. "Here we spend time with him before bed, and he still gives us a hard time. I don't know what to do with that boy."

The problem is that they failed to set the stage. Instead of preparing Jerry for bed with quiet activities, both physically and emotionally, they got him more excited and active than ever. Jerry would have been satisfied with either. What he really wanted was some time with Mom and Dad. Mom and Dad simply gave him the wrong kind of time.

And consider what that did to Jerry's self-esteem. One minute he feels like he's the most important person in the world, and the next his parents are yelling at him and hitting him. He grows confused and wonders if he should trust his feelings—and the signals his parents send.

For the sake of your child's self-esteem, when you want him to do something, set the stage first.

41—SHARE THE POWER
IN MAKING DECISIONS

Something needs to be done. Now. It affects the kids, but there's no time to involve them in the decision. Besides, they're too immature and irresponsible to really make a contribution.

Or so parents too often think.

But if they would take the time and effort to share the power in making decisions in the home, especially those that affect their kids, some wonderful things would start to happen:

The children would grow in self-esteem, since they would see that their input was valued;

The decisions would probably improve, since everyone involved had an opportunity to participate;

The children would more willingly follow through on their part of the decision, since they know they helped the family come to that decision.

Involving your child in family decision-making builds her self-esteem. She feels she's a more vital part of the family. And her subsequent actions are more supportive of family policies, giving her experiences of success.

Look at these contrasting approaches:

First approach: Father clears his throat at the dinner table. "Mark and Randy, your mom and I have decided we're going to take our vacation this year up in the mountains."

Randy frowns and says with a whine, "Mark and I wanted to go to the beach!"

Second approach: Father clears his throat at the dinner table. "Mark and Randy, I have time off in June, and we thought it would be fun to take a family vacation. What would you like to do?"

First approach: Carla is misbehaving, hitting her little brother. Mother's face gets red, and she shouts, "Carla, get up to your room! I've had it with this hitting."

Second approach: Carla is misbehaving, hitting her little brother. Mother's face gets red in anger, but she controls herself and goes over to where Carla is sitting. "I can't let you hit your brother," Mother says. "What do you think we should do to help you remember?"

42—SEPARATE THE CHILD FROM HIS ACTS

Liz has just spilled her milk all over the table. "You're so clumsy," her mother says, obviously very irritated.

Randy hits baby sister and makes her scream. "Stop that hitting," Dad says. "You're always such a brat! Why can't you be nice for a change?"

Anne has drawn a beautiful crayon picture all over her bedroom wall. Mom promptly spanks her, breaks her crayons into the trash, and shuts her in her room. "You can't come out until you've learned to stop being such a naughty girl," she says.

Sound familiar?

Liz and Randy and Anne may stop misbehaving, but most of all they'll think that they're inherently bad, which is damaging to their self-esteem.

When your child misbehaves, attack the act, not the child. Teach him that you're displeased with some of the things he does, not with who he is. Separating the child from his acts will help him salvage his self-esteem.

The distinction between *acts* and person is a vital one. When you discipline, you want to train your child to act a certain way. If you approach the problem by attacking the acts, you teach your child proper emphasis; he understands better what is wanted and why you want it. But if you attack the child himself, he only understands that he's clumsy, or bratty, or naughty.

Let's replay those first three situations to see how to deal with the act you're displeased with:

Liz has just spilled her milk all over the table. "I don't like spilled milk," her mother says. "Help me clean it up, will you please?"

Randy hits baby sister and makes her scream. "Ouch!" Dad says. "Hitting hurts! If you want to hit, punch this pillow, but don't hit your sister."

Anne has drawn a beautiful crayon picture all over her bedroom wall. "Walls are not for writing on," Mom reminds her. "Here's some soapy water and a washcloth so you can clean it up. When you're done, come down to the kitchen, and we'll color on some paper together."

43—TEACH YOUR CHILD HONESTY

Larry was crawling up onto the kitchen counter to get into the sugar bowl. He could almost taste it! Mom never let him have sugar all by itself, but it sure tasted good! He pulled open the cupboard door and reached in. In his haste he knocked over the bowl. It fell down onto the counter and broke, and sugar flew across the floor.

He was long gone when Mom came into the room and found the mess.

"What happened here?" she demanded.

"I don't know," Larry lied. When he said this, he felt a little funny inside. He felt terrible because he had lied.

"So who made the big mess and broke my bowl?" she asked.

"Maybe the cat," he said. And he felt worse.

The honest child is the one with a high self-esteem. Parents who can teach their children to be honest will be helping them to feel better about themselves.

Here are some basic suggestions about teaching honesty:

1. Always be totally honest with your child. If he knows that you've lied to him, whatever the issue, he'll come to think that lying is acceptable, even if he still feels unworthy when he does it.

2. Create a climate that is conducive to honesty. Every child is fallible, and they should be allowed the freedom to make mistakes. If they are expected to be perfect all the time, they'll simply learn to cover up their fallibility rather than learn to improve. When your child makes a mistake or has an accident, approach her in such a way that she'll know it's safe to be honest.

3. Never open the door for a lie. If you *know* your child has done something wrong, don't ask him if he did it. Simply confront him with the evidence and have it out. Don't ask, "Who did this?" Instead say, "I noticed you broke my bowl and spilled sugar all over."

4. When you suspect he's lying, tell him so—kindly. Agree that sometimes it seems easier and safer to lie. But note that it makes a person feel much better about himself when he tells the truth.

5. When your child tells the truth even when it seems hard, praise her with an I-message: "I'm happy that you decided to tell the truth even though it might have been the hard thing to do."

44—ENCOURAGE NEATNESS

"I feel better about myself when I know my house is neat and clean," says Mom.

A child feels better when he has a clean room too. The child who is sloppy and lazy about picking things up has a lower self-esteem. He doesn't take as much pride in who he is and how he appears. He doesn't feel as positive about himself.

The child who keeps things neat feels better about herself. She feels that she's worthwhile.

Parents can build self-esteem in their children by teaching them to be neat. The spirit is lifted and encouraged when the environment is clean.

When things are a mess, you get more easily discouraged. Life isn't as cheery. Everything seems to go wrong.

It's no different for a child. Self-respect goes down the drain when his surroundings aren't neat. Nothing about his life is as rosy. His self-image suffers until his environmental image is changed.

That doesn't mean that Mom and Dad have to clean up after him all the time. That's not the solution. Instead the child needs to learn to be neat on his own. The first step is to have set chores that the child is responsible for. Who cleans the child's room? Once he's four or five, he can do it by himself. Before then he can help. Who picks up her clothes? The child does. Who keeps her toys in order? The child does.

Make things easier by making the room child-sized. Put his toy shelves and clothes drawers where he can reach them. Don't use a toy box—they're unwieldy and discourage neatness. Shelves or toy bags are better.

When your child fails to do her job, don't do it for her. Don't take the responsibility from her—that will hurt her self-esteem too. Instead, tell her that she can't go outside to play until the room is clean. The job will get done.

45—TEACH YOUR CHILD TO WORK

I remember the rigors of growing up on a farm. Every morning my brother and I would get up before anyone else and go out to milk the cows—by hand. Some days we had to wade through the snow to the barn. The cows would usually be waiting by the barn door, anxious to get in. Our hands would nearly freeze while we were milking, but it had to be done. We survived.

We had a huge garden to plant, weed, and harvest, and an even bigger yard to take care of. Fences always needed to be fixed; chickens needed their daily feeding and watering (as did the cows and sheep).

Every day before and after school there was work to do. Every Saturday and all through the summer there was more work we had to finish before we could go out to play.

My parents may not have known exactly what they were doing (they probably did), but they certainly had the right idea:

The child who knows how to work has higher self-esteem. He sees how he's contributing to his family and to his world, and this makes him feel more valuable as a person.

Every young child wants to learn to work. They think it's fun to do the things that Mom and Dad get to do. Take advantage of that willingness, but don't give them more than they're ready to do. And take the training slowly; you'll have to expect a less-than-professional job for quite a while.

One thing that makes every child more willing to work is to have his mom or dad working beside him. This makes the job easier; everything seems to go smoother and faster.

Work is something everyone needs to learn to do. If you teach it to your child consistently and enthusiastically, so that he learns to be successful with work, he'll end up with a much strengthened self-esteem.

46—TEACH
YOUR CHILD FAIRNESS

Bobby wanted to play with the new toy *all* the time. It didn't matter that it wasn't his toy or that his sister Lynn wanted to play with it. All he could think of was what he wanted.

It was hard to make him change his mind. His mother tried to distract him with another toy. It didn't work. She tried to coax him, and she tried to order him. Finally, she forcibly took the toy and gave it to Lynn.

All in all, it was a bad day for Bobby. He felt as if he wasn't worth too much when Mom tried to manipulate and then force him. He felt kind of bad that she put Lynn's feelings above his.

But he felt worst of all, because he knew he hadn't been fair.

Every child understands the principle of fairness, and it becomes increasingly clear the older he gets. He understands that it's not fair for someone to have something he wants! And even though he may have a hard time admitting it, he understands the opposite—that it's not fair to others for him to have something they want.

When a child is unfair, she feels less worthy. She loses a touch of self-esteem. And if she is unfair by habit, she loses a lot of self-esteem. Parents can help by gradually teaching the underlying principles of fairness, by helping the child to see how she can put those ideas into her treatment of others.

For example: "Bobby, that's a fun toy, isn't it?" asks his mother.

"Yes," says Bobby.

"You like to play with it, don't you?" says Mom.

"Yes," answers Bobby.

"It's fun for Lynn, too, isn't it?" asks his mom.

"Yes," answers Bobby.

His mom says: "She should have a turn to play with it too.

It's her toy. Would you like to give it to her now or in five minutes?"

Even though you may never use the word *fair*, he'll get the idea. Teaching fairness is a lifetime task, and the more successful you are at it, the better your child will feel about himself.

47—TEACH YOUR CHILD SELF-CONTROL

Nate wanted a toy that Dave was playing with. He watched Dave for a minute, as the temptation grew stronger and stronger. Finally, Nate snatched the toy and ran. Dave looked up and burst into tears.

Mom came to see what the trouble was. She quickly sorted out the facts and pinpointed the cause of the problem: Nate. She gave the toy back to Dave and spanked Nate.

Moral: Nate was unable to exercise self-control, and as a result, he got spanked. Dave didn't get spanked. Nate's positive feeling about himself is diminished.

Susie was mad at Jim. He'd called her a naughty name, and she didn't like it one bit. So she hit him, hard, on the shoulder. "I hate you," she yelled, as she ran out of the room. Susie never got caught, but she felt bad because she made Jim cry. "But he deserved it," she told herself.

Moral: Susie was unable to exercise self-control and did something she regretted later. Then she tried to lie to herself about her feelings of regret, which made her feel worse. Her self-esteem shrank.

Help your children exercise self-control, and you'll boost their self-esteem. A child is like anyone else—when he controls himself, he feels better about himself. He feels more worthy about his person.

When you start to teach self-control, the place to start is with yourself. The opposite is so common it's almost a joke. It's also very ineffective: "Stop yelling at each other," Dad screamed at the top of his lungs. "I won't have any more of it!"

If the parent can exercise good self-control, he'll be in a lot better position to teach it to his children. The parent will feel better about himself, too, and will convey this to the child.

48—TEACH YOUR CHILD COOPERATION

Cooperation is the essence of a successful life. The man who's a loner and who always does things on his own has never learned to trust and work with others. As a result, he's insecure. And even though he may have all the trappings of success, he's never attained some of the more important character traits. Deep inside he's a failure.

The child who learns to cooperate with others has more self-confidence. She's able to get things done in society, not just by herself. She's able to build good relationships with others. All these lead to a heightened feeling of self-esteem.

If parents want to teach cooperation, they need to be good models. Do you constantly pull apart, working in two directions, or do you work together? The child will see your example. He'll see that as a model of how we should get along in the world.

Cooperate with your child as well. Is he trying to accomplish something? Are you working at odds with each other? Does his goal oppose yours? Get together and cooperate. Start working together so you can *both* accomplish your tasks.

Whenever your child cooperates with another, be sure to praise him in an I-message: "I'm glad about the way you and Bobby helped each other to clean your room. You both worked together to get it done—and it helped you to finish the job even faster!"

Lecturing and preaching won't do the trick. But modeling, practicing, and praising will. Your child will gradually learn the skills of cooperation.

The results will be gratifying. Things will go more smoothly in your home. Your child will feel better about himself, so much so that he'll be easier to get along with. His self-esteem will be sufficiently high that he'll be willing and able to cooperate with others as he moves outside the home circle.

49—HELP YOUR CHILD LEARN ASSERTIVENESS

We've heard a lot about assertiveness lately—probably too much. It's bred a batch of rude, selfish people.

Not everyone, of course; just those who have taken an excellent idea and gone too far with it.

Having said this as a warning, let me give you a key to building your child: **Help him learn to be more assertive. It will increase his self-esteem.**

The reason, of course, is that when a person is more assertive, she feels more in control of her environment and her life. And control leads to a better feeling about oneself.

You'll have to walk a fine line here, because assertiveness *can* lead to rudeness and selfishness. The assertiveness you teach, then, must be couched in the context of caring about others. It should be used to advance one's cause, but never to walk on others.

Compare these two approaches to assertiveness:

"Let's go play football," says Dan. "I'll be the quarterback on the first team, and Ray can lead the second team. I choose Jim and Tim and Kim to be on my team. Ray, you can have the rest."

"Let's go play football," says Mike. "We can draw straws to see who's on which team, and each team can choose their quarterback."

In both cases the child was assertive and took the lead in the situation. But the first child was just plain bossy. The second showed a willingness to work in a group situation, respecting the rights and feelings of the others.

You can teach assertiveness in many ways. The most important is to help your child understand that he should be willing to express his feelings honestly and get involved in issues he cares about. In order to teach this to him:

1. Get involved yourself. Be assertive yourself.

2. Let him express himself freely in the home, as long as he's polite about it.

50—USE A MIRROR

A mirror is a marvelous invention. And it has one exciting magical property: it's always honest with you. You may want it to show you as a movie star, but invariably it will show the truth.

Set up a mirror in your child's room. It will help him grow more accustomed to his face. It will help your child grow more comfortable with who he is. It will strengthen his feeling of self and build his self-esteem.

For example: Ronnie wasn't sure he liked his body. It seemed short and ugly. His nose was too big for his face. His feet pointed out awkwardly.

Then his parents put a full-length mirror in his room. "I don't want that old thing in here," he complained. "I have to look at *me!*"

Since Ronnie didn't like his physical appearance, he didn't want to have to look at it. Of course, in disliking his appearance, he disliked the person who went with it. He had low self-esteem.

Every morning Ronnie would get out of bed and see himself in that mirror. Every night he'd come home from school and go into his room and there was Ronnie looking at him out of the mirror.

He grumbled a bit. "Why are you making me look at *that* thing?" he asked his parents. It wasn't really a question, just a complaint, and they didn't feel obligated to answer it. Instead they countered with an observation:

"You don't like looking at yourself in the mirror, do you?"

After a week Ronnie stopped talking about it. In two weeks he hardly seemed to notice. In one month Mom noticed him one morning flexing his muscles in front of the mirror.

No, Ronnie wasn't growing narcissistic. He was simply coming to accept himself. He got used to what he looked like, and familiarity bred acceptance. His self-esteem climbed.

All from a simple image of himself, one that moved with his moves, hanging on the wall.

51—LET YOUR CHILD HAVE A PRIVATE SPACE

Ted had his own room. He didn't have to share it with anyone else and could decorate as he wished.

Tammy had four sisters. There wasn't enough space in their house to give her a room of her own, so her parents arranged for her to have a private space in her bedroom. One corner of the room was *hers*, to do what she wanted with.

Ted liked motorcycles. He got some old motorcycle posters from the local cycle shop and hung them all over his room. Dad helped him fix a little workbench along one wall, and there he put together a collection of motorcycle models.

Tammy's dad got her an old school desk from a second-hand store for only $3.50. It was exactly what she wanted. She put the desk in her corner and put all her papers inside it. A few pencils were carefully placed on top. One corner of the desk held a pretty vase of fresh dandelions. Above the desk hung a small mirror, and across the bottom of the mirror was one of Tammy's favorite sayings: "Today is the first day of the rest of your life."

Having a private space is important to your child's self-esteem. It helps the child feel she's important. It tells her that she has something all her own, to do with as she pleases.

You don't have to have a huge house to give each of your children a private space. Tammy shared her room with another sister. Every room has spare nooks and crannies. A child doesn't require much, just a corner somewhere she can call her own.

One child might have a private area put inside a closet. Let her set it up as she wishes.

Another child can have his private space in the corner of the family room. Put up a screen around his corner, and he's got his own space.

Wherever you establish a private space, observe one essential rule: keep it *private*. If it's closed off, knock before entering. Don't dictate how it's to be decorated. Don't barge in and clean up. It's the child's space, not yours.

52—ALLOW
FOR DIFFERENCES

Frank likes to play sports while his brother Hank prefers quieter activities.

Mom and Dad both enjoy sports. They play tennis together and go swimming when they have a chance. Their natural tendency is to take Frank with them and leave Hank at home because he'd rather be reading a book or writing a poem.

But Mom and Dad know that this would be damaging to Hank. It would hurt his self-esteem. It would say, "Son, what you like to do isn't as important as what we like to do. It isn't as important as what Frank likes to do." And when parents say that, even when they'd be horrified that this was the message they were sending, it's only a short step for the child to start thinking: "What I like to do isn't important. I must not be important."

To build your children's self-esteem, allow for differences in how they approach life, in what they like to do with themselves. Consider both differences between themselves and between them and you. Plan activities that will satisfy the needs of all.

Be honest about those differences. Your child's choice, whatever it is, is valid. Acknowledge this, then plan activities that will help him participate more fully in that choice.

For example: "Let's all go play some tennis," say Mom and Dad. "Hank, we want you to come play too. We like you to be with us, even though you've said you don't like tennis. Then after we play a game or two, let's go over to the library. Frank, maybe you can find a book on horses, since you're interested in them. And we can all enjoy a quiet hour just browsing through the stacks."

Every person is unique. You as parents may end up with children who are completely different from you. Acknowledge those differences; acknowledge that they're valid. Plan for activities that will help you all appreciate the differences together—and this will help your child know he counts!

53—SHOW ACCEPTANCE BY LISTENING PASSIVELY

It's easy to talk to your child when he comes to you with a problem or complaint. But it's harder to sit silently and listen "passively."

You've heard the definition of a good conversationalist: "someone who lets the other person do all the talking." That's exactly what you should do with your child.

Passive listening can be a powerful tool in building your child's self-esteem. By listening to his concerns without judging or criticizing, you show him that his feelings are valid and are worth being heard.

Henry C. goes to see a psychiatrist. "I don't even know why I'm here, Doc," he says. "I'm not even sure I have a problem."

"Uh-huh," the psychiatrist says.

Says Henry: "I really don't have much of anything to say. I don't know what to say."

Then Henry spends a full hour telling the psychiatrist his life's history with little more feedback from the doctor than his occasional "Uhmm," or "Uh-huh," just to let Henry know the doctor was still with him.

When Henry walks out, he feels renewed and refreshed. "It was great," he tells his wife.

What did the psychiatrist do that worked so well? He let Henry talk. His noninterference in the conversation let Henry know that what Henry had to say was important and worth hearing.

You can do the very same thing with your child, especially when you know that what he really needs is just to talk about his problem.

"Dad, I have a problem at school," says Kathy.

"Yes," says her father.

"It's this other girl," says Kathy. "She calls me names. The other day she . . ."

Kathy doesn't want advice. She doesn't want her father to tell her what to do. She wants to be *heard* and understood. By listening passively, her father will give her what she needs.

54—FIND THE POSITIVE UNIQUENESS

Christine was incredibly smart. She was always ready with the right answer in class. The teacher was really excited to have Christine in her class. "This child's a *genius!*" she said.

Stanley was creative in his play. What he did wasn't so unique, but what he *said* he was doing showed an impressive imagination.

Julie was very helpful at home. All her mom had to do was say, "Julie, can you help me with . . . ?" and Julie was busy doing what needed to be done.

However, Christine had a hard time getting along with other children. Stanley was nervous and withdrawn, and he wouldn't go out to play with others. Julie was intelligent, but somehow she couldn't get good grades at school.

The parents of these children could try to attack the problem: "Stanley, you really need to play with other kids," says his father. "I'm going to take away your blocks for the rest of the day, and I want you to go play with Pete next door."

But in attacking the surface problem, they'd be dealing only with a symptom, not the real problem. This is because Christine and Stanley and Julie, and millions of other children like them, aren't suffering from unsociability or meanness or lack of intelligence. Their real need is higher self-esteem. Once that need is met, the other problems will gradually disappear.

So how do the parents build their self-esteem? Easy:

Find the positive uniqueness. Focus on that. Show the child how good he is at some things. Help him transfer that feeling to other activities.

"Christine, the teacher tells me you're one of the best students she's ever had," says her mother. "I'm happy with how well you're able to do your assignments." Nothing is said about play with other children. The focus is on the things Christine does well—the things that make her unique in a positive way.

55—LET YOUR CHILD GROW AT HIS OWN RATE

Stella wasn't walking yet, and she was already eighteen months old. Her mother and father grew increasingly concerned. There were several other babies in the neighborhood, all younger than Stella, and they *all* were walking.

What could be wrong? Finally, her mother consulted with the doctor. He assured her that *nothing* was wrong and that she shouldn't be concerned.

Mother was comforted for a while. Then the little boy next door, only nine months old, started to walk.

"Nothing's wrong with Stella," her mother thought. "The doctor said so. And I'm going to teach her to walk!" She started to have daily sessions with her baby, walking with her, cajoling her, trying to bribe her to walk on her own.

The sessions grew increasingly tense. Soon Stella's mother was yelling and spanking, but Stella still didn't walk without hanging on to something.

And something worse began to happen. Stella began to cry more often, over nothing. It was harder to get her to flash that cute smile. She seemed less sensitive to what was going on around her.

Stella was gradually losing her self-esteem. She didn't understand everything that was going on, but she did know that her mother wasn't happy with her, so Stella couldn't be happy with herself.

Let your child grow at his own rate. Every child has a different speed of development. It's helpful to know typical progression rates and typical learning levels. But these are only guides. Let your child grow at her own rate, and you'll protect her self-esteem.

Stella's mother should back off. Stella's not walking yet because she's not ready to walk yet. Other children younger than she are walking, but that shouldn't matter a bit.

Child development progresses by levels. If a child hasn't finished the things she needs to accomplish at a given level, she'll stay at it a while longer. Accept your child's unique growth pattern, and your child will feel more accepted as a person.

56—TEACH RESPECT FOR THE CHILD'S CULTURE

The Hispanic child has a culture that may stem from Mexico, where people have a different type of culture than the homogenized one in the United States. Their art is different, and even the media their artists work in is different. They have a different lifestyle and a different outlook on life.

Some blacks point with pride to their African heritage, but most of the present black culture comes from centuries of slavery in the South. This culture is reflected in their songs, their writing, and even some of their older idiomatic expressions.

American Caucasians come from a number of different countries. One may be from Norway, another from Italy, a third from Australia. Each "mother" country gives its children a different base culture.

Some parents are uncomfortable with their heritage. They're happy to have finally blended with their fellow Americans in every way; their dress, speech, home, and lifestyle are all identical with their neighbors'. Often the only difference one can tell between one person and the next is the last name or perhaps the color of the skin.

Ignoring heritage and culture is a mistake. Teaching your child about her cultural background is a good way to boost her self-esteem. It shows her some positive ways in which she's unique. It helps her to be proud of her family name and all it represents.

A study among the American Indians has shown that many Indians have a low self-esteem. This is because they are uncomfortable with their heritage and want to deny it. In doing so, they deny themselves.

Build your child's respect for his culture, and you build his self-esteem. Heritage is inseparable with one's feelings about oneself.

57—TAKE PICTURES

Pick up your family album and leaf through it often with your children. There's Annie with her front two teeth missing. "Remember how you lost those Annie?" asks Mom. "You fell on the steps and screamed until we came. We were worried that something awful had happened, but it was only your teeth. The new ones grew back in and everything was okay."

Josh is in the picture below her, his arm around his dog. "He sure was a great dog, wasn't he, Josh?" says his dad. "You taught him some great tricks. I've never seen a dog stand and dance better than Benny could. And you really took good care of him. He'd be so sad when you left for school each morning, and I'm sure he perked up and heard you coming when you were still three blocks away after school was out in the afternoon. Benny was a special pet. I still miss him."

On the next page you see the whole family, standing together in the backyard. "That was taken last summer," recalls Mom. "Boy, that was a busy day, wasn't it? There in the corner you can see the garden that Josh helped me plant. And Annie helped to keep the weeds out of it. I think we got some of the best corn I've ever tasted out of that garden. Let's plan an even bigger one for this year."

Your child's self-esteem will grow if you take his picture often and review those snapshots together frequently.

Taking someone's picture tells them that they're important to you and that you want to be able to look at them even when they're not around.

Even if the child doesn't stop to think about it, he'll get a real boost.

58—ENCOURAGE A JOURNAL

Dear Diary:
"Today I really got in trouble. Mom got mad at me. I went to Pam's house without asking, and Mom told me she'd had it with me and I was grounded. She didn't spank me or anything, but I thought she would. I guess she was right to be mad."

"Dad took me to the zoo today. He said it was our date. We bought some popcorn to eat while we looked at the animals. I saw lions and tigers and bears and polar bears and monkeys and giraffes and ostriches and antelopes and zebras and hippopotamuses and gorillas and goats and flamingoes and leopards and fish and turtles and some other things. Dad bought some peanuts out of a machine for us to feed to the monkeys. I ate some too."

"I'm happy. Mommy read some fun stories after lunch. She told me about when she was a little girl. She had FIVE sisters. Mommy was the smallest. They fought sometimes, but they were happy lots of times."

Encourage your children to have a journal, diary, or personal record. Such a record will help them have a better feeling for themselves; their self-esteem will grow as they see they have personal thoughts that are worth recording. And as they review their journal from time to time, they'll gain vital perspective.

What things can you do to encourage a journal?

A good first step is to keep one yourself, which will show your children that parts of our lives are worth keeping a record of.

Second, help your child purchase a notebook or diary to keep his thoughts in. Help him think of things to record, but only for the first few times. After he gets the hang of it, let him be on his own. What should he record? Most important are his *thoughts* and *feelings*. Next come special experiences. Then everyday experiences.

Third, if your child is interested, include journal-time in your daily routine with him.

Fourth, be sure to let the child keep his journal *completely private*.

59—SHOW YOUR CHILD YOU CAN BE TRUSTED

When Tommy hurts his knee, he runs into the house for comfort. His mother or father is there to offer comfort— to give a hug, wipe the tears, give a kiss, wash off the wound, or put on a psychologically healing bandage. Tommy learns to trust them.

When he has something exciting to share, most people in the world won't listen to him, but Mom and Dad do. They're willing to take a moment and talk to him, to hear what he has to say. Sometimes they're too busy, but then they say, "I really can't stop this now. Can we talk in ten minutes?" Mom and Dad always hold true to their promise; in ten minutes they take time to talk to him. That builds trust.

When Tommy had a fight in the schoolyard with another child, he was worried about what his parents would say. He knew he might be punished, but he knew he could trust his parents to not overreact, or, on the other hand, to act as though they didn't care at all.

Every Friday night Mom and Dad go out to eat or to a show. They leave Tommy with a baby-sitter. He's not afraid or worried, because they always come back. He trusts them, and they have earned the trust.

Sometimes Tommy really makes a mess, and sometimes he gets so upset that he throws things all over the floor. What do Mom and Dad do? Usually they punish him. And there Tommy trusts them too. He knows that they've set limits, and that they care enough to stick to them. But he trusts them never to abuse him. He's never been abused, and he doesn't even know about the word or the concept. He trusts them to treat him right. And they do.

There are many ways we can show our children that they can trust us. Tommy's parents show us a few of those ways, and I'm sure you can think of many more on your own. Be consistent, be loving, be honest about your feelings, be honest about your mistakes, and above all, help your child feel secure with you. These things will build a feeling of trust in the child.

Trust is essential in a young child (old ones too). They help the child feel like she has a place of value in the world. The result is a strong self-esteem.

60—SHOW YOUR CHILD YOU TRUST HIM

Trust is the ultimate act of love. When you trust someone, you tell them you believe in them and have confidence in them

You can see the effect of trust on self-esteem. When others have confidence in you, you're only a step away from having confidence in yourself, and self-confidence is a prerequisite and companion of self-esteem.

The more your child feels you trust him, the more he'll trust himself, and this will help his self-image to grow increasingly more positive.

Trust creates great expectations. The person who is trusted knows that something important is expected of him. He can let the other person down, or he can live up to the expectations. The choice he makes, whether consciously or subconsciously, will determine how he feels about himself.

Your trust can build your child up to previously unknown heights of self-confidence and self-competence.

But your trust must be *appropriate*. If you trust your child to do things he's unable to do, you're placing unrealistic expectations on him. And that will *tear down his esteem*.

"I'm going to lock myself in my study to get some work done," says Dad. "I trust you and your sister to not make any messes." (If a child needs to be reminded not to do something, he's not ready for the heavy weight of trust.)

"I trusted you to tell me the truth, and now you've lied to me," says Mom. "I'm really disappointed in you." (Children under the age of eight have a relatively undeveloped view of right and wrong. These are areas of *hope* and *instruction* but not of trust.)

Where, then, does trust come in? In simple, yet important ways, where the word *trust* is usually unspoken:

"You're always willing to love me."
"You're always willing to forgive me when I make mistakes."

"You really try to please me."

A child is immature and often unable to control his actions, principally because he can't even understand them. But we trust him. We trust him to try to make the right choice, and this parental attitude does much to build self-esteem.

61—ACCEPT YOUR CHILD'S SEXUALITY

Carl is sitting quietly at the kitchen table cutting out paper dolls. He carefully cuts out each doll, then proceeds to cut out the clothing and accessories that go with the dolls, until his mom comes in the room.

"Don't be a sissy, sitting there playing with paper dolls!" she says. "Why don't you go out and ride your bike with your friends?"

Wanda is outside playing in the mud, making little mud pies and lining them up on the sidewalk. Her dress is covered with mud, and when her mom sees her, she gets upset.

"That's no way for girls to act!" she says. "You'll grow up being a tomboy. *Girls* don't play in the mud and dirt. Now get in here and clean up before I spank you."

Something's wrong here, and it's not with the kids. No, Carl won't grow up to be a homosexual. No, Wanda won't grow up not fitting in with other girls. It's natural and normal for children to experiment with all aspects of life including those that may not fit into their parents' preconceptions of masculinity and femininity.

If these mothers continue to try to fit their children into a sexual/gender mold, the result will be a loss of self-esteem.

Build your children's self-esteem by letting them explore and experiment with their surroundings, whether they're trying "boy" things or "girl" things.

They'll settle down into something close to the traditional sex roles soon enough. But in the meantime, let them learn all different kinds of things. It will help them broaden their horizons, and it will help them feel better about themselves as persons.

62—HELP YOUR CHILD HAVE A HEALTHY VIEW OF SEX

"Mommy, where do babies comes from?" asks Mary.

"Don't bother me now. I'm busy." Mommy says.

"Mommy, where do babies comes from?" asks Mary again.

"The stork brings them," replies her mother.

"Mommy where do babies come from?" asks Mary.

"God sends them to earth," says her mom.

"Mommy . . .?" asks Mary.

Take a deep breath and think about what your child is really asking: "Mommy, where did I come from? You and Daddy are big and you've always been together, but I know I wasn't always here. I came later. How did I come here? Why did I come here?"

Teaching your child about sex and reproduction is much more than simple instruction in the facts of life. It's a great opportunity to tell your child how he or she fits into the joy of being a family and the deep pleasure that comes from sharing a life with him.

But watch out. If you're uncomfortable with a discussion of sex, your child will think that something's wrong. Two negative results:

"The body is bad. *My* body is bad. I'm bad."

"Maybe something bad happened to make me come here."

Build your child's self-esteem by conveying a positive attitude about sex and sexuality. This will help him feel better about his body, and it will help him know that he plays a vital and important part in the family.

Sex is hard for some of us to talk about. Here are some keys:

1. Be honest. Tell the truth. Treat reproduction as something that's a normal part of human life. Don't load everything on your child at once; take it a step at a time, responding honestly to his questions. Then about the time your child starts first grade, you might want to give him an overview.

2. Be positive. Have a good attitude about sex. If you have negative feelings about it, your child will pick them up. That's inevitable, so be honest again: tell your child that you're uncomfortable talking about it. Tell him that's a problem with you, not with the subject.

3. Take the opportunity to teach morality. Teach your child what you expect of him morally. Your expectations will be another boost to his self-esteem.

63—HELP YOUR CHILD "OWN" HIMSELF

Laurie was playing in the bathroom sink. The plug was in, and the water was creeping closer and closer to the top. It was fun. Laurie put more and more toys in the water, and each time more and more water sloshed onto the floor. She played for a half an hour there, while Mommy was taking a nap, then finally got bored and went on to something else.

When Mommy woke up and saw the mess, she was furious: "Laurie, you were supposed to be taking a rest in your room. And look what you've done." Water was all over the bathroom walls and floor and all over Laurie.

Laurie stuck out her pretty bottom lip and pouted: "I didn't do it, Mommy. I was in here playing, and the water just splashed out onto me. I didn't make it splash."

Laurie knew she made the mess, of course, but she didn't want to *own* the problem.

Ownership of one's body and what it does is crucial for a child (adults too!). The child who owns himself has high self-esteem. The child who refuses to accept responsibility for himself has low self-esteem.

Parents can help their children have high self-esteem by helping them to own themselves.

"Laurie, you know as well as I do that water can't jump out of the sink all by itself," says her mother. *"You made it splash."*

Parents can help the child accept responsibility for his acts simply by refusing to let the child weasel out. When the child tries to pawn off ownership of a problem, the parent can confront the child with the truth, not in an accusing or condescending way, but simply by stating the facts.

However, parents shouldn't be overly harsh on the child by unduly punishing her, and they shouldn't worry that the child is becoming a liar. Just acknowledge to the child that you know better, and then take the necessary steps to correct the situation.

"You made this mess while I was sleeping," says Laurie's mom. "No one else was around to do it. Now I want you to clean it up. Here's a towel. When everything's dry, you can come down and be with me."

64—BE ON GOOD TERMS WITH YOUR SPOUSE

The parents' relationship with one another affects how a child feels about himself. For instance:

1. The family is the center of the child's universe. That universe is held together by his parents—both of them. When parents fight or bicker or simply treat each other unlovingly, the child begins to question the security of his world.

2. Too often the child feels he's at blame when parents fight, especially if he hears them fighting *over him*. The result: the child feels less worthy, since he feels that he is causing disharmony in the world of the home.

3. Children learn by modeling. The child who sees her parents repeatedly communicate in unloving ways learns to communicate with others in the same ways. This kind of communication is never satisfying, and the child never feels good about herself.

Be on good terms with your spouse, and you'll build your child's self-esteem. Be on bad terms with each other, and you'll tear it down.

It would be unrealistic to expect all couples to always get along with each other. Parents are going to continue to fight even when they know their child's self-esteem is at stake.

But here are three important points:

First, try to make the *bulk* of your communication positive. Sure, you'll fight and be negative with each other, but try to make that the exception rather than the rule.

Second, when you fight, stick to the issue at hand. Try to deal with that issue, rather than using it as a springboard to attack each other.

Third, whenever possible, fight in private. You'll certainly have disagreements in front of your children, but when you do, make sure they see you make up as well as fight.

65—HELP YOUR CHILD BE A FRIEND

Few things are more damaging to self-esteem than the feeling that one is unloved and unwanted.

Few things can help one feel loved and wanted more than to be friends with someone your own age.

You can help your child be a friend. The more capable she feels in friendship, the better she'll feel about herself.

"Everybody hates me!" Anita cried. "No one wants to play with me."

As her mother discusses the problem with Anita, she discovers that Anita always insists on having her own way. Certainly that's the wrong approach if one wants to have friends, but the problem is particularly difficult with children. Anita thinks her peers don't like *her*, not considering that it's her *methods*, not her*self*, they don't like. With that feeling, her self-esteem shrinks.

That's where a parent comes in. Children are often selfish and self-centered, which are part of growing up and discovering oneself. The actions that build good friendships don't come naturally for all children, but parents can help children learn them.

Here are some basic rules:

1. If you want to be accepted and included, accept and include others. "I'll bet that made Charlotte feel really bad when you said that you didn't want to play with her," says Anita's mother. "How do you think you can include her next time?"

2. Those who do things for others learn an "other-attitude," and they generally make better friends. "Randy really needed help this morning, didn't he?" says Dad. "And everybody just laughed at him. How do you think you could help him out tomorrow?"

3. Friendship doesn't always come easily. One must often keep trying. "I know that Jeff is rude to you and teases you," says Steve's mother. "But what will happen if you keep trying to be his friend?"

66—HELP YOUR CHILD GET INVOLVED

A school-age child needs a lot of peer involvement. It boosts his morale, and it helps him feel that he is an acceptable person. In fact, it gives him regular reminders that others like him and are pleased to be associated with him.

Such reinforcements, of course, are very supportive of a healthy self-esteem. They tell your child that he's a likable person and that he fits in with others.

What can you do to help in this process? You can help your child get involved with groups of children his own age.

The more positive associations a child has with his peers, the better he will feel about himself.

You can help your child enroll in classes he enjoys.

You can help him join sports teams he's interested in.

You can get him involved with a group his age at church.

You can help your child join a boy or girl scout troop.

You can take your child and his friends on outings to the park, the zoo, a ball game, or the ice cream parlor.

You can encourage him to invite others over to play.

You can be willing to let him go to others' homes to play.

Experts have shown repeatedly that this kind of peer involvement is essential to the normal development of a child. It helps her learn all kinds of vital social skills that she'll use throughout her life.

You've seen the child who doesn't fit in. He doesn't really know how to interact with others, because he hasn't had enough experience. And he has low self-esteem. Let your child spend time with others his age, and he'll learn the skills he needs to get along in life, and at the same time his self-esteem will grow.

67—HELP YOUR CHILD
BE A PROBLEM-SOLVER

Holly comes home from school crying. "Ella says she hates me," she sobs. "She doesn't ever want to talk to me again."

"There, there," her mother says. "Here's what you can do . . ."

Our children's lives are filled with problems. Some seem small and insignificant to us; others we agree are major. But, large or small, they have a multitude of problems *every day*.

How should a parent help her children with their problems? The question is an important one, because if the parent does either too much or too little, she's doing the child a disservice.

Here's what happens. If the parent steps in and takes over, the child thinks that she's incompetent to solve her own problems. Down goes the self-esteem.

If the parent acts uncaring, the child thinks her problems don't matter. Again, down goes the self-esteem.

When your child has a problem, guide her as she reaches her own solution. This approach will build her esteem; she'll see that you view her as capable and that you feel her problems are important.

How do you act as guide? Help your child find the basic issues of the problem by asking questions:

"Why do you think Ella is upset?"

"Do you really think she'll still be mad tomorrow—or next week?"

"What do you think will help her feel better again?"

"What are some other approaches you could try?"

By using this question method, you're able to show your child you care without directly intervening. The child still comes to her own conclusions and must act on her own to carry out the solution.

68—FIND A MODEL

As a role-model for your child you show him how people are expected to behave in our society. Children learn by watching and observing, and if they have good models to copy, they'll be able to adapt to society quite well.

This leads to greater self-esteem. When a child is able to fit into his societal surroundings, he feels better about himself.

But there's often a catch. Your child needs a model that's the same sex as he is—and what if there isn't one in your home? Despite a lot of the media hype we've had in the past few years, there really is a difference between boys and girls. Neither is smarter than the other, but their physical and emotional make-ups are different.

The boy who doesn't have a man to look up to feels uncomfortable with himself. He's unsure around others. When he interacts with other boys, he's often a little hesitant.

The same applies, of course, to girls.

How can you find an acceptable model for your child if there isn't one in the home? There are a lot of places you can look:

Your brothers or sisters
Your parents
Big Brother
Big Sister
Boy Scouts
Girl Scouts
Community sports
Your clergyman or women's group leader
Church groups
Neighbors
Community education.

Remember one important thing: you need to be a good model for your children yourself. Your search for an additional model to help your child feel comfortable with his sexuality should start only if yours is a one-parent home and if your child is of the opposite sex.

69—LET YOUR CHILD
BE HIMSELF

"I can't see how you failed to make the team," Dad says. "You're big enough. You're good and strong. I think I'll go have a good talk with your coach."

You can tell Dad is disappointed. What you can't tell is that he's much more disappointed than he's letting on. The issue is deeper than the fact that his son failed to make the football team. The real problem is that Dad always wanted to play football and couldn't. "But at least my son can," he reassured himself.

And now his son can't.

Dad is suffering from a lack of self-esteem. He feels a giant gap in his life. He doesn't feel as important as he would like to. But if his son were to excel, he'd feel a lot better.

What about the son, though? He has his own life to live. He may not be suited for the goals that his dad sets for him.

Don't use your children to fill gaps in your own life. Don't use them to make up for your own lack of esteem. Let your child be himself.

Sometimes this is pretty hard for a parent who feels that he doesn't have a lot of value as a person.

If the parent has low self-esteem, the child will probably have low self-esteem too, and children with low self-esteem seldom excel.

The parent finds himself in a vicious cycle, and the solution is for him to build his *own* self-image, on his *own* terms. He needs to accept the positive things others see in him. Then he won't need to rely on his children for gratification, and only then will they be able to give it.

70—AVOID LABELS

You can call your child *honey* and *sweetie* and *cutie pie* and *sugar* and *pal* and *son* and whatever other good things you can think of, but never attach a negative label to your child.

Negative labels destroy self-esteem, and too often the child starts to believe them.

The result becomes a sort of self-fulfilling prophecy. If you call your child a "brat" often enough, pretty soon he'll believe you. And as a result, he'll *really* start acting like a "brat."

Avoid these negative labels and any others you might call your child:

lazy
slowpoke
blockhead
dumbo
stupid
brat
creep
dummy
bully
selfish
messy
loudmouth
fatso
pest
crybaby
whiner
sassy
dirty
obnoxious
rude
spoiled
liar
ding-a-ling.

71—AVOID PUT-DOWNS

Nothing is more devastating to a child than to have his parents put him down.

"You never do a job right," says Joe's father.

"Don't go correcting your little sister—you don't know *anything* yourself," says Pat's mom.

The ego is a fragile thing. In a child it's especially fragile, closely tied to his parents and what they say and do. When a parent puts her child down, at the same time she puts the child's ego down.

And what is the ego? A big part of it is a person's self-image and how he views himself.

When a child's parents put him down, he usually has only two reactions, both destructive. He may have a strong enough ego that he refuses to believe them, and the rift between parent and child widens. Or he may be at a stage of his personal development where he *does* believe them, and to believe a put-down is to deny your own self-esteem.

Don't put your children down. Build them up, and you'll build their self-esteem.

Begin by noticing the good things about your child. Comment on them. Praise him for the things he does well.

But whatever you do, don't put him down. When you put someone down in any area of his life, you put him down in his self-esteem.

72—GIVE IMMEDIATE POSITIVE FEEDBACK

A dog always knows where he stands with his master. When the dog is learning new tricks, the master uses a system of rewards to train him. For example, if a dog is learning to roll over, his master will give him a reward when he lays down. When the dog rolls partway over, he gets another reward. When he rolls all the way over, he gets a *big* reward.

And he gets a lot of attention and affection from his master while he's learning. The only input he gets is positive. If he fails to roll, the master doesn't spank him and say, "Bad boy!" Instead the master works with him *positively*, and when the dog finally performs, he gets immediate positive feedback.

Certainly our children are much more complex, much more intelligent, and much more important to us than dogs, but there are a few things that parents can learn from a dog trainer. One of the most valuable is the principle of immediate positive feedback.

Children thrive on attention, and they invariably get a sense of satisfaction in pleasing their parents. But too many children don't have any idea what it takes to please their parents; they only know what upsets them.

As a result, they never really know how best to fit into their parents' universe. They know what doesn't work, but they don't always know what *does* work. *They don't know where they stand.*

When people aren't sure how they fit in with people important to them, they question their own validity as a person. They wonder if that individual called *me* is good for anything at all, and their self-esteem suffers.

You can make sure your children don't suffer from this problem by giving them positive feedback when they do something well—and giving that feedback immediately. You'll build their self-esteem, because you'll be teaching them how they relate to you.

73—LOOK FOR THE GOOD

Melissa cleaned off the table after supper. In the process she scattered crumbs all over the floor, she lost a spoon under the refrigerator, and she broke a dish in the sink.

You might say her effort was a *total* disaster, but Melissa's mom is particularly wise. She knows that if you criticize a child when she's trying to help, she won't be particularly eager to help the next time.

The solution, then, is for Mom to find the good in what Melissa has done. "Melissa," Mom says, "you sure did a great job of scrubbing the table."

Melissa beams: "I'm sorry I messed everything else up, but I did a good job there, didn't I?"

Kids know when they've done something wrong. They don't need to be reminded—or lectured—about that. But they're unsure about when they do something right, and that's when Mom or Dad comes in and looks for the good.

In looking for the good in your children, you'll be building their self-esteem. You'll help them see that they have worth, and that even though they aren't perfect, at least they can do some things perfectly.

74—TEACH MORALITY

A good sense of morality helps a person have strong self-esteem. He can better understand his place in society and his relationship with his fellow man. He can better understand the effect of his actions on those around him, and he seeks to conform his actions to their greatest benefit.

Henry found a $20 bill on the grocery store floor. He took it to the manager and said, "I'll give this to you in case someone comes forward to claim it. If they never do, you can give it back to me." His act of simple morality helped Henry feel good about himself. He felt like he had worth and value as a person.

James was having a hard time with a test at school. He hadn't studied enough, and he just couldn't figure out the answers. Finally he leaned over, very quietly, and copied the answers from the girl next to him. When he handed in the paper, he knew he'd get a good grade, but he didn't feel very good about what he'd done. He felt cheapened, like he was less of a person than he'd been the day before.

Teaching your children simple morality will help them develop a strong self-esteem. Moral children like themselves better than those who don't have high values.

How do you teach morality to your children? The first and most important step is to exemplify morality in your own life. If your child sees that *you* are "morally straight," she'll be much more inclined to be that way herself.

If you're a church-goer, you'll find that your local church will help you in your effort to teach your children morality. Take advantage of the opportunities your church offers.

Finally, help your children know that you value morality by teaching it to them directly and positively reinforcing them in their actions when they choose the moral path.

75—LEARN ABOUT CHILD DEVELOPMENT

Warren and April were playing together, and suddenly Warren hit April. He took her toy and walked away from her, while she began to cry.

"I'm so sorry," Warren's mother said to April's. "Warren's going through another stage."

There *are* definite stages of child development, and we can know a great deal about our children by knowing what stage they're in. If we know where our children are in their development, we can know what to expect of them.

Having reasonable expectations of a child is vital to his self-esteem. If a parent expects too much, the child will feel incompetent and incapable. If the parent expects too little, the child will feel unloved. An awareness of the stages of child development is vital to an effort to build self-esteem.

There are many good books available on the stages of development, and I recommend the following:

The Child Under Six, by James L. Hymes, Jr.; Prentice-Hall; Englewood Cliffs, NJ; 1963.

Childhood and Adolescence, by Joseph L. Stone and Joseph Church; Random House; New York, NY; 1957.

Infant And Child In The Culture Of Today, by Arnold Gesell and Frances Ilg; Harper & Row; New York, NY; 1943. Also by the same authors and publisher: *The Child From Five To Ten* (1946), and *Youth* (1956).

Books with helpful sections on child development include:

How To Parent, by Fitzhugh Dodson; New American Library; New York, NY; 1970.

Your Child's Self-Esteem, by Dorothy Corkille Briggs; Doubleday; Garden City, NY; 1970.

76—GET TO KNOW YOUR CHILD

It seems like such an obvious thing to say: "Get to know your child." Yet it's advice that must be given, because many parents don't naturally learn who their children are. Maybe the reason for this is that it's not an easy job. Children change from month to month (the Terrible Twos, the Thoughtful Threes, and the Fearsome Fours seem to describe them week by week, not year by year), and it's hard to keep track of exactly where your child is at any given time.

Knowing your child is vital if you hope to build her self-esteem. Only then will you know what kinds of expectations to have, and remember that a child feels good about herself only when she meets your expectations.

There are many ways to learn who your child really is. The most important two are *listening* and *observing*.

Listening. When your child has something to say to you, take time to listen. If you can't really *listen* right then, tell your child, and make a point to listen later. When you listen, hear the words he's saying, and read between the lines. Ask yourself, "What is he really telling me?" "What does he really want me to know?" "What is he feeling now?" "What does he want to feel?"

Observing. Watch your child throughout the day. I'm sure you have a good idea of his activities and behavior, but spend some time watching him just to learn more about who he is. How is he at mealtime? Naptime? How is he when playing with others? How is he when playing by himself? How does he handle new situations? How does he deal with frustration?

By learning more about your child, you'll be able to be more accurate in the expectations you set for her. By setting reasonable expectations, you can help create success experiences for your child every day, and experiences of success are the basis for self-esteem.

77—LET YOUR CHILD GROW CREATIVELY

Every person in the world has a creative streak in him. Just look at your child's drawings. Chances are they'll be as free and natural as Picasso's—and in some ways as exciting. That's not because Picasso wasn't any good. It's because your child has inborn creativity.

Maybe your child's strong point isn't drawing. Maybe it's in his use of words, either written or spoken. Maybe it's in the way he puts his blocks together or the way he moves.

Whatever your child's creative bent, if you encourage it, you'll build his self-esteem. Creativity is an area where a child can excel on his own terms. It's an area where you can be supportive—and excited with him. Most important, when your child creates, he draws something from within. And when you encourage this, you tell your child that he, as a person, is valuable and important.

Creativity is closely tied to self-esteem. Encourage creativity and you build your child's feelings of self-worth. Ridicule or ignore your child's creative efforts, and you make him feel rejected.

How do you foster creativity?

1. Be interested in what your child is doing. Ask her about the projects she chooses to get involved in. *Listen* to her answers.

2. Be as excited about impromptu projects as more involved ones. Your child will express his creativity as much in a road in the sandpile as in a three-dimensional model made from scratch.

3. Watch for those areas your child seems to be naturally attracted to. If she seems to be physically oriented, her creative talent might be in sports or dance. Encourage participation or classes in these areas.

4. Sometimes a child expresses creativity simply in the way he approaches life: he may ask a lot of questions or seem particularly curious. If this is the case, be patient and responsive.

5. Finally, try to get your child involved in activities other

than watching TV. Television, despite its many positive points, can discourage creativity. And if your child isn't being creative, you lose a great opportunity to build his self-image.

78—ENCOURAGE THE USE OF IMAGINATION

"Mommy, I saw a giant outside!" says Tim. "He was taller than the house. His teeth were giant! I thought he was going to eat me up, so I ran and hid!"

"When I grow up, I'm going to be Roy Rogers," says John. "I'll ride a big white horse, and I'll kill all the Indians."

What do you do when your child says these kinds of things? Do you stifle the use of his imagination?

For example:

"There's no such thing as a giant," says Tim's mother. "Now you stop saying those kinds of things."

"You can't be Roy Rogers," says John's dad. "There's only one in the whole world and he's already himself. Besides, I don't like you to go around talking about killing Indians."

A child's view of himself is closely tied to his imagination. Crazy ideas come to him just like they do to an adult, but there's one big difference: the child is less experienced. His mental visions are more real to him than they are to you, and he's less hesitant about expressing the wild imaginings that come to him.

When a parent tells his child in unspoken, subtle ways that her imagination has no value, the child begins to feel that you're attacking her and her worth.

It's easy enough to let your child's imagination go. It will be active anyway. **You can build his feelings of self-worth by having fun with it, by encouraging him to use it:** "A giant! What color was he?"

79—ADMIT IT WHEN YOU'RE WRONG

When I was younger, I had a friend who was *always* right. His father was the same way as he was. It didn't matter what the issue was. His dad had to be right, every time.

It might seem that this friend and his dad had a high self-esteem, but actually the opposite was true. They both suffered from a feeling of inferiority and from a lack of confidence. Their show of *over*confidence was all a cover-up.

If my friend had learned that it's normal to make mistakes, he could have built some self-respect on a more reliable foundation. But he wasn't getting much help from home.

If you don't acknowledge your mistakes, you do your children a great disservice. Such an approach will give your children a false view of life. They'll think that mistakes are something bad, and when they make a mistake, they'll think that they're not valuable people.

You can boost your child's feelings of self-worth if you admit it when you make a mistake. This will show him that mistakes are acceptable in life and that when he makes one he's not so bad after all.

You don't have to be infallible to your child. By being fallible and acknowledging your mistakes, you teach your child important things about how life really is.

80—FREEDOM TO FAIL

Children need to understand that failures and mistakes are a part of life. The person without failures never grows and never learns to truly appreciate life's triumphs.

Allow your child to fail, and you build his self-esteem. He'll fail whether you like it or not, but he'll be greatly strengthened if he knows you support him in failure as well as in victory.

It's easy to be supportive of someone who has just won. Everyone likes a winner, but it's the loser who needs the support. Your child needs to know that you're proud of him when he does well. But, even more, he needs to know that you accept him complete with failures and mistakes.

Ellie was baking cookies by herself for the first time. She made a mess in the kitchen and burnt the cookies.

"Messing up the kitchen like this just isn't to be tolerated!" says her mother. "Now get busy and clean all this up."

Try again, Mother. **Mistakes are a part of life and must be tolerated.** A child's self-esteem is infinitely more important than any mess or failure.

"You made cookies all by yourself?" says Ellie's mom. "That's fantastic! Let me try one. It's kind of hard, isn't it? What do you think happened? I think it's great that you were willing to try this and next time it will be easier."

Ellie knows that her effort wasn't successful. Her mother doesn't have to tell her that, but she does have an important message to send: I love you even when you fail. I accept you even when you fail. You're important to me even when you fail.

81—EXPRESS YOUR FEELINGS HONESTLY

If you learn to express your own feelings honestly, your child will learn to do the same. He'll learn that his feelings have validity, and that it's legitimate to express them. He'll learn that negative feelings do not make him unworthy. He'll feel better about himself, and he'll have a better self-image.

In a make-believe kingdom, the king proclaimed that no one would be allowed to express any negative feelings. "Negative feelings are a sign of weakness," the king said. "And I'll allow none of my subjects to be weak."

The people grumbled, privately, about the new rule. "What if I really do feel bad?" a woman asked her husband.

"The king says that no one really ever feels bad," he answered. "They just *think* they do."

So the people obeyed the decree, fearing to do otherwise. But though they never felt any bad feelings, at least so they were told, their faces grew long and their frowns grew deeper.

The old men died younger and younger. The children grew up without smiles or laughter, and even the sky seemed less blue.

"We have the most positive-thinking kingdom in the entire world," the king bragged.

But it was also the least happy. In denying their "bad" feelings, the people denied *themselves*. And emotionally, at least, they withered and died.

Whether they are positive or negative, feelings are good for the human soul. A parent teaches this when he expresses feelings honestly. A child can see that feelings are important in life, and that his feelings have value. If his feelings have value, then he must have value too!

82—CUDDLE AND CARESS YOUR INFANT

Several years ago in Russia, scientists conducted a study with two groups of infants. Infants in the first group were diapered and fed, but they received as little human contact as possible. The second group was given the same physical treatment, but they also recieved a lot of physical affection.

The results of the study are quite predictable. The second group flourished. Infants in the first group grew sickly, more prone to disease, and totally disinterested in their surroundings. Some literally gave up and died.

The scientists concluded that good physical contact is a matter of life or death for a baby.

Cuddling and caressing a child also have a marked effect on his self-esteem. The baby who is given a lot of affection makes much more rapid progress than the baby who isn't. The baby who's been cuddled feels more secure and more important.

Start to build your child's self-esteem from the day he's born. Show him you love him and care about him by cuddling and caressing him often.

When you feed your baby, hold her close.

When she's awake and alert, play with her fingers. Kiss her on her forehead. Tickle her toes. Let her touch your face.

Talk to her. Tell her you love her. She'll get the message.

83—GIVE PLENTY OF AFFECTION

Nothing beats a good hug! "Hi, Mom. I'm home," says Sally. She puts her lunch pail on the kitchen counter and starts to go upstairs.

But Mom stops her, puts her arms around her, and gives her a big hug. "Did you have a nice day?" asks Mom.

Sally smiles widely and hugs her mother back.

Our children have a never-ending need for affection. It's one way we tell them that they're important to us and that we're willing to reach out and include them in our lives.

Physical and verbal signs of affection are among the most important things we can do to build a child's self-esteem.

There are many ways we can show affection. The first is a hug, often accompanied by a kiss. Touching in general is a good way to show affection. Rumple your child's hair, hold her hand, squeeze him on the shoulder, tickle her, wrestle on the floor. Let him sit on your lap.

Parents can help their children learn to express themselves by being affectionate in the home, and dads should be sure they get involved in these physical displays of affection too.

While you're showing affection, don't forget to verbalize it too. "I love you." "I'm sure glad you're in our family." "Thanks for being you." "I like it when you give me such a big hug. Can I have another?"

84—DO THINGS TOGETHER

We're all so busy that sometimes we forget the most important thing in our lives—other people. And the most important people, of course, are our own children.

It's essential to spend quality time with your children. By spending good time with them you increase their feelings of self-esteem.

The first problem, of course, is how to find time. Those who are most successful at doing things with their children regularly have found that it helps to have a set time every day for "time together." The child knows when the time is and looks forward to it.

How do you make your time together worthwhile?

First, let your child choose what he wants to do. Whether it's coloring together or reading a story.

Second, have a set length of time for your time together. Try setting a timer for that length of time, and play until the timer buzzes.

Third, remember your child has a short attention span. Be willing to switch activities if he gets bored.

Fourth, take special pains to avoid having an unhappy experience with your child during your time together. Refuse to give him a payoff if he acts up. Instead say, "I'm sorry you decided to scream because you broke your crayon. It's hard to have time together when you're screaming so that's all the time we'll spend today. Maybe tomorrow you can remember not to scream."

85—SHOW INTEREST IN YOUR CHILD'S ACTIVITIES

When your child comes home from kindergarten with a bunch of papers, you look at them and show him that you're interested in what he's done and how well he's done it.

But what do you do when he brings them home ten days in a row and each day is just a repetition of what you've seen before?

To build your child's self-esteem, show a genuine interest in his activities, even if they do seem tiresomely repetitive. If your child is excited, be excited with him.

How do you get excited about the same thing ten times in a row? Your child's excitement is the key. He's excited because the activity is still new and fun for him. Try to empathize with his feelings, and he'll know you care.

Show your interest by asking questions. For example: "I like the colors you used in this picture," says Tom's mother. "Can you tell me about it?"

"How many flowers did you draw in this picture?" asks Billy's dad. "Can you count them for me?"

"Did your teacher ask you to draw a horse, or did you decide for yourself?" asks Julie's mother.

You should also show interest in activities your child does around the house. Use the same approach: empathize with how he feels and show your interest by asking questions.

When your child draws a picture or builds a castle or constructs roads in the sandpile or learns to somersault, let him know that you're interested. This will make him think that he's someone important.

86—"UNIMPORTANT" PROBLEMS

Diane can't make the pieces of her puzzle fit together. Ronnie loses his truck in the sandpile. Alan falls on the sidewalk and scrapes his knee.

Your first instinct is to ignore a child when he or she has an "unimportant" problem. But for a child, every problem is very important.

Build your child's self-esteem by showing her that the things that are important to her are also important to you. Let her know that you care about the things she cares about.

For example: "Puzzles can be frustrating sometimes," says Diane's mother. "Let me help you find the right pieces."

"That's too bad about your truck, Ronnie," says his mother. "Let me finish the dishes, and then I'll come out and see if I can help you find it."

"Let me see your knee, Alan," says his dad. "I'll wash it off for you."

There is a possibility that you can turn your children into crybabies by sympathizing with their every little problem. The key is to determine the times when the child really cares about the problem and when he's trying to manipulate you to get your sympathy.

By caring about the "unimportant" problems in your child's life, you show your child how much you love him.

87—GIVE YOUR CHILD
THE ATTENTION
SHE NEEDS

Melanie stands at her mother's legs and whines.

Troy throws a temper tantrum on the living room floor.

Jackie tosses food off her tray and squeals.

"Just ignore them," says Mom, "They only want attention."

Mom's assessment is probably correct, but the children need attention as much as they need food and shelter. When a child doesn't receive enough attention, she misbehaves.

The prime people who give a child attention before she starts school are her parents. If they give her too little, the child begins to think she's not *worth* attention, and her self-esteem goes down accordingly. You can't give a child too much attention, because no matter how much you give, there's always room to receive more. She can never get an overdose.

To build your child's self-esteem, give her all the attention you can.

This doesn't mean that every time your child misbehaves you give her more attention. Teach your child to express her need for attention in acceptable ways. For example: "You're whining around my legs because you want attention," says Melanie's mother. "Attention is a good thing to have, and I want to give it to you. If you can play quietly in your room for five minutes, then I'll come up and spend some time with you."

Or: "I can't spend time with you right now because it's almost suppertime, and I've got to get everything ready," says Troy's mother. "Would you like to get a chair and watch me?"

88—LOVE EACH OF YOUR CHILDREN FOR HIMSELF

Vanessa and Bryan are fighting again. "You're stupid because you won't let me have that truck," Bryan says.

"I'm not going to play anymore," Vanessa says.

"Give me that truck, or I'm going to tell Mommy," says Bryan.

Much has been said about sibling relationships and sibling rivalries, and there are two principles that are true:

1. Children sometimes feel that they're rivals for your love. They're very sensitive to a parent's fairness. It's easy for them to feel that they're not getting the love and attention they should be getting, especially when it seems like a brother or sister *is* getting that attention.

2. Children need yardsticks by which they can measure their own worth and capability. Often the most convenient yardstick is a sibling, and each child ends up comparing himself to a brother or sister, which is destructive.

Parents can have a great influence on potential sibling problems. **When each child knows that his parents love him for himself, he develops high self-esteem.**

Bryan runs to his mother and says, "Mommy, Vanessa's being mean to me. She's naughty. Give her a spanking." Bryan's not asking for his truck here. What he really wants is for his mom to demonstrate to Vanessa that he's more important than she is.

But Mom doesn't accommodate him. Instead she shows both children that she loves them for what they are, each as a unique individual. "Bryan, you're so good at building things with your blocks," says his mother. "Could you make something for me? Vanessa, I need a new picture to hang on the refrigerator. Could you draw one?"

By emphasizing what each child does well, Mom's able to defuse the situation. She's able to show each child that she loves him or her not by choosing sides in an argument but by pointing out her children's different skills.

89—COMMUNICATE LOVE, NOT JUST THE TRAPPINGS

Some parents communicate the words of love but not the trappings. Some have the opposite problem, and they communicate the trappings but not the love.

What are the trappings of love? The words, hugs and kisses, pats, and time spent with the child.

It's possible for a parent to give all those *trappings* to a child without ever actually communicating love itself. For example:

Miriam sits on her mother's lap while she reads her a story. Mom holds her close and occasionally gives her a hug. "It's good for me to do this," Mom thinks. "Miriam will know for sure that she's important, that she's loved."

Miriam enjoys the experience, too, but the story is hard for her to understand. "What's a bugbear, Mom?" she asks.

Then in the next sentence, she asks another question. Her mom quickly grows exasperated and says, "Do you want to hear this story or not?"

They read on and Miriam begins to squirm. "Sit still!" her mother says.

If a parent is going to take time to show love to a child, it only seems reasonable that the child will be polite and attentive in response. This may be reasonable but is not very likely. A child comes from a different world than you do. Her perceptions are different. When you show her love (and that should be all the time), you need to do it on terms that she'll understand. Holding the child close and reading a story is great, but when the child grows tired of the activity, love her enough to switch the activity.

If you want your child to have a high level of self-esteem, show her real love, not just love's trappings.

The best way to do this is to communicate on her level. Let your expressions and evidences of love fit *her* needs, not yours.

90—LET YOUR CHILDREN LOVE YOU

Everyone agrees that it's important to show love to children, and studies have shown that when a child doesn't know he's loved, his view of the world becomes distorted. He becomes a nonachiever, and he's unable to cope with difficulties.

But there are two sides to love. We should show our children that we love them, and we should also allow our children to show love to us.

The child who knows he's able to love feels that he's a valuable part of society. He has high self-esteem.

Consider how *you* feel if others tell you they love you. When they want to, they show physical affection: hugs, kisses, and pats. When they want to, they say, "I love you. You're important to me." You start to feel pretty good.

But they never let you initiate the expressions of love. "I love you," you say.

"Sure," they answer. "Later. . ."

You try to give them a hug. "Not now," they say. "I'm busy." You don't feel very good about not being able to express your feelings, and this applies to children too. For example:

When her dad comes home after a hard day at work, Cindy waits at the door. "I love you, Daddy," she says. "I'm sure glad you're home."

Her father says: "Let me relax a few minutes and read the paper before you talk to me."

Cindy's self-esteem goes down. Can this be the same father who is so loving and affectionate, she wonders.

Children often choose bad times to show their love, but we need to let them show it *when they want to*. After all, that's what *we* do.

91—LET YOUR CHILD MAKE MISTAKES

Joy is building a "tower" with her blocks. The building grows taller, and her mother is sure it's going to topple any minute so she steps in to help: "Here, dear. If you just move these two blocks this way, and if you put this top one here instead of here, the tower will work."

Alice is coloring at the kitchen table while mom fixes lunch. She turns the page and picks up a blue crayon to color a vase full of roses. "Honey, use the red crayon," she tells Alice.

When you don't intervene in your child's activities and allow him to do things his own way, even if it means he makes mistakes, you show him you accept him. And this kind of acceptance leads to self-esteem.

It's hard not to intervene. You want your child to learn how to do things right. You want him to excel. You want to feel needed.

But usually it's best just to leave the child alone. Smile and talk to him, but don't talk about the project until it's done. Then you can praise a part of the project your child did well: "You stayed in the lines really well when you colored those roses," says Alice's mother.

"Wow, that tower is almost as tall as you!" says Joy's mom.

It's more important to allow your child to try things her own way than to make sure that she does it right.

92—SEND NONVERBAL MESSAGES OF ACCEPTANCE

Sometimes parents *think* they're showing their child that they accept him as a person, when actually they're communicating the exact opposite.

For example: Larry's dad is watching a TV show when Larry comes running into the room. "Hey, Daddy. Guess what!" says Larry.

His dad wants Larry to know that he is more important than any television show, so he turns to him and says in an animated voice, "What, Larry?"

Larry immediately launchs into an enthusiastic tall tale, and his Dad pretends to listen. He nods, says "uh-huh" at the appropriate places, and usually looks at Larry. But his eyes keep darting to the TV show that is on.

Larry finishes his story, but he leaves a little less enthusiastically than he had come. His dad has sent him nonverbal messages of nonacceptance.

For your child to have a high self-regard, your every communication must speak acceptance, both verbal and nonverbal.

Larry's father communicated nonacceptance, although he didn't realize it. There are other nonverbal ways of communicating nonacceptance: not looking at the child while you talk to him, using facial expressions that show boredom or irritation or frustration, and assuming a posture that leans away from the child.

We need to show nonverbal acceptance: look at your child with a steady gaze, smile, use facial expressions that show love and interest, and a posture that leans toward your child.

You don't have to do a scientific study to know what kinds of nonverbal messages you're sending. Here's your key: in all your communications with your child, make sure you think, "I love this child. I care."

93—PUNISH RESPECTFULLY

This sounds like a paradox, because punishment doesn't usually come packaged with respect.

But it's not impossible to do both simultaneously. Many parents learn to do it expertly, and in the process they strengthen the bond with their child and help the child know that he's someone important and valuable in their lives.

Disciplining with respect goes a long way toward helping a child have self-respect. He sees that you value him and learns to value himself too.

Disciplining with respect means treating your child as an individual with rights and privileges, recognizing that your child has feelings, and acknowledging his need to learn from mistakes.

Most of us have tried at one time or another to discipline a child by using a threat, but threats have three problems. The first is that they don't work. The second is that we're then backed into the corner with a threat we can't carry out. The third is that it shows a lack of respect for the child. It shows her that we don't trust her to obey without severe punishment and that we don't think her feelings or needs are worthy of consideration.

Threats are only one way we show lack of respect. Others include yelling, hitting, being rude, refusing to listen to the child and being harsh.

Treat your child with respect, and you'll get respect back. Build your child's self-esteem, and soon she'll choose to listen to you because she knows that makes her feel better about herself, not because she's afraid of you.

Respect is mutual understanding, willingness to listen, being polite even in discipline, giving the benefit of the doubt when appropriate, and recognizing that your child has needs and feelings too.

94—GIVE CHALLENGES

Steve rips the wrapping from his birthday present. He pulls out a box, and his eyes grow wide: "Oh, boy," he says. "An airplane model!"

Steve's never put a model together before, but he thinks he can do it and he's willing to try. It will be a challenge. But if it were too easy, it wouldn't be any fun.

One way to build your child's self-esteem is to give him challenges. Challenges help him develop his abilities and help him prove to himself that he's a capable person.

Don't just give challenges haphazardly, though, because you can do more damage than good. If you give a child a challenge that's too much for her, you *destroy* her feelings of self-worth. She thinks that she's let you down. She thinks she wasn't as capable as she should be, and her self-esteem goes down.

To make sure you give the right kinds of challenges to your child, follow these three simple rules:

1. Challenge her in areas where she's already demonstrated strength.

2. Make sure he's interested in the challenge. Don't just pick something you'd like to see your child do; pick something *he'd* like to do.

3. Make the challenge a little difficult, so that it *will* be a challenge, but not so hard the child will be afraid to give it a try.

95—DEALING WITH DISCOURAGEMENT

The discouraged child is one who doesn't feel good about himself. He doubts his competence, his ability to *do*, and he doubts his own value as a part of his environment.

What are the signs of discouragement? A child who is discouraged simply gives up and says, "I don't want to." "I can't." "It's too hard."

There are other telltale signs. If your child withdraws from others, if she mopes around, if she gets obviously upset about the project or task she's trying to handle, she's probably discouraged.

Help your child overcome his discouragement in productive ways, and you help boost his self-esteem.

For example: When Hal gets discouraged, his father helps him understand his feelings. "You feel unhappy because this job seems too hard for you," says his dad. Then his father helps him find his own workable solution.

"Maybe if you tried it a different way it would work for you," says Hal's dad. "What do you think might be a good way?"

His father reinforces his success, even if it was only partial: "Hal, it was good that you were able to pick up all those clothes so fast. That bedroom looked like it would be hard to clean, but you got right in there and picked up all of your clothes."

Discouragement often comes in small portions, but don't ignore these problems. Help your child to deal with small problems, and he'll gradually acquire more and more ability to successfully deal with the many challenges he faces every day.

96—INVOLVE YOUR CHILD IN CONFLICT RESOLUTION

Consider these two scenarios:

Scenario 1

"Janet, you can't get up from this table until you eat your peas!" says her father.

"I hate peas!" answers Janet.

"Well," says Dad, "you have to eat them. They're good for you."

"I don't want to eat them," says Janet. "They make me sick."

"Listen, young lady, either you eat your peas or you get a spanking," says Dad.

Replies Janet: "All right! But I hate peas, and I hate you too."

Scenario 2

"Janet, you can't get up from this table until you eat your peas!" says her father.

"I hate peas!" answers Janet.

"Well," says Dad, "you have to eat them. They're good for you."

"I don't want to eat them," says Janet. "They make me sick."

"Listen, young lady, either you eat your peas or you get a spanking," says Dad.

Replies Janet: "I don't care. I'm not going to eat them."

When a conflict arises, involve your child in its resolution. You'll get much better results, and the child's self-esteem will grow. Letting the child participate in the solution to the problem will tell him his views are important and so is he.

Let's look at a third scenario:

Scenario 3

"Janet, are you getting up from the table?" asks her father. "You haven't finished your peas."

"I hate peas!" answers Janet.

"Well, it would be best if you ate them," says Dad. "It's better for your body if you eat some of everything your mother prepares."

"I don't want to eat them," says Janet, "They make me sick."

"We've got a problem here, don't we?" says her father. "I'd like you to eat your peas because you need the variety, and you don't want to because you don't like them. What should we do?"

"Well, maybe I could just eat two bites," answers Janet.

"Will you eat two bites?" asks her dad.

"Yes, I could do that," says Janet, who eats two bites and then goes outside to play.

By involving your child in conflict resolution, you get a solution that's acceptable to all involved. In addition, your child feels much better about herself.

97—TEN NONCOMMANDMENTS OF COMMUNICATION

Much of the way our children feel about themselves comes from how we communicate with them. **If you want your child to have good self-esteem, communicate with him honestly.** Here are the ten noncommandments of communication, ten things you should *not* do if you want your child to have a good opinion of himself:

1. Don't give orders or commands. This type of communication tells the child that you don't care about what he feels or needs and that you only care what *you* feel or need.

2. Don't threaten your child. Threats make the child resent you, and they cause the parent-child relationship to deteriorate. Since you're the child's prime source of self-esteem, his view of himself also deteriorates.

3. Don't preach. Preaching may cause the child to think he's "bad," or it may make him feel his parent doesn't trust him.

4. Don't give advice. Advice tells a child that you don't feel she has the ability to solve her own problems.

5. Don't judge or criticize. Criticism belittles the child and his self-esteem.

6. Don't ridicule. Ridicule tells the child that you don't think she's very important or very capable.

7. Don't analyze. Analysis suggests you don't believe in your child's feelings or that your judgment is superior to hers. It suggests that you are more important as a person than your child is.

8. Don't sympathize. Sympathy generally cuts off any further communication, and it suggests to the child that the matter is closed.

9. Don't interrogate. Interrogation cuts off further communication; it tells your child that you want to control what he talks about and that you don't care about what he really wants to say.

10. Don't joke or change the subject. This kind of communication tells the child you don't understand him.

98—UNDERSTAND THE MEANING OF "I CAN'T"

"I *can't* tie my shoes," says Beth. "It's too hard." "I *can't* clean my room," says Tim. "It's too messy." "I can't get this toy to work right," says Pam.

Our homes are full of can'ts. They show up on every side. And every one of them is another brick thrown against our child's self-esteem. Sadly, it's the child himself who usually does the throwing.

Help your child understand the difference between can't **and** won't. **Help him understand that she's as capable as she lets herself be, and you bolster her self-esteem.**

No one feels good about himself when he's constantly faced with things he's unable to do. Every new obstacle is another blow against his feelings of self-worth.

But what if he suddenly discovers that his inability to perform comes by choice, not by inherent lack of capability? Just as suddenly he becomes master of his environment.

How do you help your children understand that they have this kind of control in their lives? The most important thing you can do is give a lesson in semantics. Our words limit us, but when we change our vocabulary, new horizons suddenly open up.

For example: "The toy will work right, if you take the time to learn," says Pam's mother.

"If you would like to learn to tie your shoes, I'll help you learn," says Beth's father.

"You can clean your room, even if it's messy," says Tim's mom. "Do you mean that you're choosing not to?" When he says yes, he acknowledges his competence.

Can't and *won't* are two very different concepts, but it's easy for a child to confuse them. Help your child know the difference, and you strengthen his self-esteem.

99—SHOW ACCEPTANCE BY LISTENING ACTIVELY

Sometimes your child needs the kind of support passive listening can give him. He needs to be *heard* and doesn't really need your input in his problem.

But other situations call for a more active response. The best approach to active communication is called active listening. Active listening is simply rephrasing the things your child tells you. It reassures your child that you *are* listening and tells him he's worth listening to.

Active listening is an approach that builds your child's self-esteem. It shows you accept her and her feelings.

For example: "Mom, I'm having a hard time in school," says Anita.

"You're finding school difficult," says her mother.

"Yes. It's math," says Anita. "I hate it."

"So you're having a hard time with math," Mother nods.

"It wouldn't be so bad, but the teacher gives us so *much* work," answers Anita. "I can't keep up."

Says Mom: "You find it hard to do all the math you get assigned."

"I feel dumb because none of the other kids are having a hard time," says Anita.

Through active listening, you get to the real problem. As Anita's mother listens, she gradually learns that the real problem isn't difficulty in math or assignments that are too big. It's a feeling of inferiority compared with other children.

Children need parents to *listen* to them. They need to know that their parents understand and still accept them. Active listening is a great builder of self-esteem.

100—AVOID COMPARISONS

"What's the matter with you, Nancy?" asks her mother. "Betty would never mope around like that! Now dig in and get those dishes done!"

"You should be ashamed of yourself, Vicki," says Dad. "Your big brother *never* got a C on his report card. What's the matter with you?"

"Why can't you be more like June?" asks Mom. "She never leaves her room messy!"

Start comparing your children with one another and two things happen:

1. Improvement *doesn't* come.

2. The child who's on the negative end of the comparison loses self-esteem.

Never compare your children to one another. It will squelch their self-esteem. It will make them think that they're unworthy.

How does it feel to be unloved? Just ask a child whose parents subject her to comparisons all the time. The parents never say, "I don't love you." In fact, they may often voice the words, "I love you."

But whenever they make a comparison, they send a louder message: "However much I may love you, I love your sister (or brother) *more*. Your sister (or brother) is so much more worthy of love."

That's a heavy burden for a child to carry. And it all comes from being compared with someone else.

Comparisons are unfair in a deeper sense too. Each individual is unique. Each person has her own strengths or weaknesses. When a parent makes comparisons, he negates that uniqueness. He says, "We're going to ignore your differences for now. We're going to ignore your strengths and look only at your weaknesses. And we'll look at those weaknesses from the point of view of your sister's strengths."

Nothing could be more unfair. And few things are more damaging to self-esteem. "My love is conditional," the parent seems to be saying. "My approval is conditional. And here is the condition: perform like your sister. Be like your sister. Conform to your sister's example."

Let each child be unique. Let each child be himself or herself. Avoid comparisons.

101—COMMUNICATE EFFECTIVELY

Few things tell a child how his parents really feel more thoroughly than their methods of communication. There are so many ways communication can be done poorly or not at all.

Communication that helps a child know he's important is communication that will build his self-esteem.

Here are several things you can do to help your child know she matters to you:

1. Give your child the time she needs to express herself. To do this, you have to really want to hear what she has to say.

2. Have an honest desire to help him. If your child approaches you at a genuinely bad time, tell him that you see he's upset but that you can't talk to him right away. Tell him that, as soon as you can, you'll discuss the problem.

3. Accept your child's feelings as genuine, no matter how alien they are to you. You can't dictate what or how he should feel, even if you try.

4. Don't be concerned about your child's strong negative feelings such as hate or despair. Feelings change quickly for adults as well as for children, but don't tell your child this to cheer him up; instead empathize with what he's feeling *now*.

5. Let your child know you trust her to work out her problems. Let her know that you are available, but she also needs to know that you have confidence in *her* abilities.

6. Recognize that your child has his own life to live. If you hold him too close and believe that your success or failure hinges on how he does, you'll convey that in your communication, and he'll hesitate to tell you how he feels.

ABOUT THE AUTHORS

Child psychologist Alvin H. Price, Ph.D., is author and co-author of eight books about child development and family relations. He is a professor of child development and family relations at Brigham Young University in Provo, Utah, and a consultant to the National Head Start Program, the U.S. Office of Education, and school districts throughout the United States. Dr. Price is also a member of the National Follow Through Evaluation survey team, a select group of educators who visit, evaluate, and upgrade child development and family relations educational programs at colleges and universities throughout the country.

Jay A. Parry is the author of more than a dozen books and the former associate editor of a national family magazine. As a lay church worker, he has counseled hundreds of parents in parent-child relations.